Diane Nares is the co-founder of the Emilio Nares Foundation, a non-profit charity which provides transportation and other vital support to families who are navigating through their child's journey with cancer. Nares expresses her passion for life in a wide range of pursuits, from comforting parents who have lost their child, to participating in family bereavement groups, to hosting ENF's annual food & beverage fundraiser. Born in Los Angeles, Diane Nares is a "self-proclaimed" later-in-life wife and mother to her only child, Emilio. Emilio lost his life to leukemia shortly before his sixth birthday. In addition to being a respected speaker, Nares enjoys traveling internationally, swimming, yoga, cooking, and hiking with her husband, Richard.

To my husband, Richard; and my son, Emilio, who gave me the strength to breathe again and endure each new day.

Diane Nares

HIS PLACE AT THE TABLE

A PERSONAL, PUBLIC, AND SPIRITUAL LOVE STORY

AUSTIN MACAULEY PUBLISHERS™

LONDON • CAMBRIDGE • NEW YORK • SHARJAH

Copyright © Diane Nares 2023

All rights reserved. No part of this publication may be reproduced, distributed, or transmitted in any form or by any means, including photocopying, recording, or other electronic or mechanical methods, without the prior written permission of the publisher, except in the case of brief quotations embodied in critical reviews and certain other non-commercial uses permitted by copyright law. For permission requests, write to the publisher.

Any person who commits any unauthorized act in relation to this publication may be liable to criminal prosecution and civil claims for damages.

All of the events in this memoir are true to the best of author's memory. The views expressed in this memoir are solely those of the author.

Ordering Information
Quantity sales: Special discounts are available on quantity purchases by corporations, associations, and others. For details, contact the publisher at the address below.

Publisher's Cataloging-in-Publication data
Nares, Diane
His Place at the Table

ISBN 9798886938470 (Paperback)
ISBN 9798886938487 (ePub e-book)

Library of Congress Control Number: 2023905239

www.austinmacauley.com/us

First Published 2023
Austin Macauley Publishers LLC
40 Wall Street, 33rd Floor, Suite 3302
New York, NY 10005
USA

mail-usa@austinmacauley.com
+1 (646) 5125767

I am completely grateful to everyone who has been a part of this book. Your wisdom and belief in this story gave me the strength to see it through, particularly in the painful moments of remembering.

To my Cappetta siblings, you are my tribe. My sister Teresa Kaupke, my brothers, Michael and John Cappetta, and our sisters Patty Perkins, and Nancy Casey, who both left this world too soon. Once we were six, now we are four; I treasure each of you and your spouses in my life.

To my entire Cappetta, Nares, and Anderson family; my deepest respect and gratitude to you all for loving Emilio so much, and for picking Richard and myself up, every time we fell.

To my publisher, Austin Macauley, it has been an honor and a joy to work with your amazing team who, together, made it possible for my book to become a reality.

To my editors, Patty Testerman, Debra Ginsberg, and the talented Elizabeth Ireland, each of you opened my eyes to the truth that my book needs to be in the world and that it can make a difference in the lives of so many people who have suffered a catastrophic loss. You gave me the confidence to believe that I had a compelling story to tell, and that I could write it.

To San Diego community leader, Patty Brooks, who along with my extended family of friends, neighbors, and the San Diego community, rallied around our family throughout Emilio's cancer treatments. Thank you, Patty, and so many others who researched on our behalf, assisted us in creating the largest bone marrow drive in San Diego, those of you who cooked us hot meals, walked our dog, Sierra, and so much more, thank you for your unwavering faith in our journey and ultimately in this book.

To the skilled and compassionate Hematology-Oncology team of Rady Children's Hospital San Diego, the Dana Farber Cancer Institute and Boston Children's Hospital, all of whom not only took impeccable care of Emilio, but also, the two of us.

A blessing to all of those individuals at the Emilio Nares Foundation who keep our mission and vision alive and moving forward. Program Director – Luz Quiroga, the devoted ENF Staff, and Board of Directors.

Most importantly, to my husband Richard Nares, my love, my life partner, my reason for surviving our greatest loss, I love you Emilio's father, forever and always.

Table of Contents

Prologue	**11**
Chapter 1: In an Instant	**13**
Chapter 2: I See You	**20**
Chapter 3: At the Core	**29**
Chapter 4: Challenges and Blessings	**42**
Chapter 5: The One	**54**
Chapter 6: Family Approval	**68**
Chapter 7: Wedded Bliss	**71**
Chapter 8: And Then There Were Three	**75**
Chapter 9: Our Little Fighter	**83**
Chapter 10: A Divine Friendship	**87**
Chapter 11: Remission Is a Good Word	**96**
Chapter 12: Our New Tribe	**109**
Chapter 13: San Diego's Poster Boy	**115**
Chapter 14: A Familiar Journey	**120**
Chapter 15: Entering a New Domain	**127**
Chapter 16: The Donor Search Begins	**131**

Chapter 17: The Possibility of Hope	**143**
Chapter 18: A Second Chance	**146**
Chapter 19: Freedom in Boston	**157**
Chapter 20: A New Birthday Begins	**160**
Chapter 21: Angels in the Hallway	**170**
Chapter 22: Home Without Emilio	**184**
Chapter 23: And Then There Were Two	**186**
Chapter 24: Throwing It All Away	**196**
Chapter 25: Active Healing	**207**
Chapter 26: Kitchen Table Conversations	**212**
Chapter 27: How It All Began	**217**
Chapter 28: Richard's Epic Runs	**225**
Chapter 29: Those Who Do the Healing	**232**
Epilogue	**236**

Prologue

Looking back, I realize that my whole life pivoted around my memories of those individuals who inspired me with their strength in the face of adversity. We all ache and crumble on those days when our world falls apart. The question becomes, "What do we do in the moments that follow our disappointment?" The action we take is what truly marks our path to healing and our eventual return to peace.

In this book, I weave in pieces of my life before my husband Richard and my son Emilio entered it. As a young woman in my twenties and thirties, I was obsessed with the constant need to further my education, return to my European roots, and work through the adventurous, challenging, never-dull restaurant industry.

My eventual desire to meet my life partner and hopefully have a family of my own led me from the all-consuming restaurant industry straight into the career of my dreams, representing wineries from all over the world. Ultimately, I was blessed with the chance to become a mother. When I held my son Emilio in my arms for the first time, I finally understood that he would define what my life would become.

This book speaks volumes about the power of community, family, and deep friendships, but my story's heart and soul are a collection of memories of my life with Emilio. Throughout the following pages, I will share with you the many lessons he taught me. I eventually became someone other than who I thought I was. I became someone more authentic, more alive, and more present.

One of my sweetest memories was when I worked from home and was able to witness Emilio at play. We bought him a jeep when he was five. Rosa, his nanny, would take him up and down the alley outside my office window. My mood always brightened, and I smiled every time I heard the sirens from Emilio's jeep and the turning of the big, powerful wheels. Sierra, his dog, would prance alongside him as she protected his every move. I was certain he felt proud and accomplished while driving his jeep and commanding the road! Perhaps he understood that moments such as these were one of the few times he could control anything about his life.

Throughout my time with Emilio, I began to understand that grief and joy are intertwined and exist within and apart from one another.

May Emilio's story bring comfort to those who suffer and inspiration to those searching to live their lives with truth.

Chapter 1
In an Instant

The pediatric oncologist paused for a moment, gazing deeply into our eyes as he stumbled to get his first few words out coherently. Both my husband Richard and I stared back at him, speechless.

"I'm sorry to tell you this, Mr. and Mrs. Nares," Dr. Sudari said. "Emilio's blood tests confirm that he has leukemia." Emilio was our only child. He had just turned three years old. In the time it took for the doctor to speak these words, our lives were changed forever.

In an instant, I found myself not only unable to move but unable to speak. I could not find the language to express my pain. My mind raced back to the doctor's three words, "Emilio has leukemia." As I attempted to stand up, I fell to my knees, screaming my son's name.

Emilio was not in the oncologist's office. When we arrived that day, a nurse had immediately enticed him to join her in the nearby playroom.

I could not contain this horrible information or the rush of emotion I felt.

I understood nothing about his words, not just because I didn't know what leukemia was but because my entire body and mind had shut down.

All I remember was melting into Richard's solid and broad shoulders. I wanted him to rescue me from this appalling, incomprehensible news.

"Please," I pleaded. "Tell me this is just a bad joke!"

Richard couldn't tell me that. He, too, couldn't get the words out. His facial expression glazed over with the same heavy grief I felt.

What seemed like hours later, although it was only a few moments, I felt the warm arm of a nurse wrapping herself around my upper body. What was happening in that room was as if a tsunami had blown in from the open window and flooded the doctor's office. I remember thinking that perhaps this compassionate nurse was stepping in to rescue me before I could be washed out to sea. Finally, Richard and I could fully reach our arms out to one another as we collapsed and became one. Tears were pouring down our faces in an endless stream of anguish.

I sat helplessly, waiting for some sense of order to take over. Each new word I heard, leukemia, oncology unit, white blood cells, sent a dagger to my heart.

I have always needed a sense of order in my world. It is my nature to want to control everything, especially when it came to protecting my child. There is nothing about childhood cancer that makes sense.

My mind wandered to the countless people who do not care for their children properly—the parents who communicate by screaming or ignoring their children altogether. I could not allow myself to think about the many parents who abuse their children and scar them emotionally and physically for life.

All of the above scenarios are the opposite of how Richard and I cared for our son. From the first moment we laid eyes on Emilio, our hearts were no longer our own. We were transformed and immediately head over heels in love with him.

I quickly moved my thoughts beyond the reality that there were undeserving individuals gifted with children and started obsessing about the myriad of guilt I was experiencing. I could not stop asking myself, "Why my child? What did I do wrong in my pregnancy?"

I blamed myself for swimming regularly in San Diego Bay, where the naval vessels docked and moved in and out of the harbor. I grew angry thinking about how I would occasionally spike my morning decaf with the leaded stuff to get me through the workday while pregnant with Emilio. Or perhaps it was the many tastes of Burgundy, Barolo, Chianti, Sangiovese—you name it—that I consumed in my wine industry career well before Emilio came into my life.

The most haunting question I couldn't shake off was, "Did my only child get leukemia because I was an older mom?" I gave birth to Emilio when I was 42 years old. I waited a long time in my life to have a child. As the eldest of six children, I didn't grow up dreaming about marriage and having a family of my own. I wanted to pursue my dreams of going to college, traveling to Europe, and having a career. In 1970, when I graduated from high school, my aspirations weren't the norm. Many of my friends searched for the perfect husband and settled in a house in the San Fernando Valley of Los Angeles, where I was born. I always felt guilty that I didn't dream about having babies.

Guilt crept in as I blamed myself for being so selfish. "Older eggs, damaged eggs?" I asked myself.

"Where was the doctor!" I cried out. "I have so many questions I need to ask him!" I continued to shout these words to whoever would listen. I had a desperate need to resolve the turmoil and the all-consuming fear that was raging within my mind. At the same time, I became aware that my body was slipping into a tidepool of grief. A feeling of complete and utter sadness stayed with me that day and the many days that followed.

I couldn't get rid of the horrific thought that it was possible to sit down on the floor one evening to play with Legos and then, the very next morning, receive a call that meant life would never be the same again. There was something ominous lying-in wait.

The events that led us to that paralyzing morning with Dr. Sudari started a few months prior. Cancer is typically lurking in the body long before its diagnosed. Blood traverses, cells appear and die, and proteins form for consumption. Our bodies are constantly working invisibly to us until the moment something goes wrong. In the case of Acute Lymphoblastic Leukemia (ALL), one sinister cancer cell appears. It slowly grows, joins the dark side, and becomes Darth Vader, destroying healthy cells within the body in a deadly pas de deux. This alchemy of destruction is often a long process, at least six months, while the cell's host is unaware of the demolition within.

After kicking off winter with constant colds, I thought I'd better take Emilio to the doctor. It seems simple, but the tricky part is when you say, "My child is always sick. What is wrong?" maternal anxiety often gets brushed aside by pediatricians because colds are so common among preschoolers. There is a constant baton pass of kids bringing germs into and out of the classroom.

We reluctantly agreed to "just wait it out." Doctor's orders.

It was a rough holiday season, and Emilio's third birthday came up right away in early January. Our sweet little boy, stricken with another terrible cold, looked miserable. We threw his birthday party at the San Diego Children's Museum. After the party, we dined with everyone at one of our favorite restaurants, Pizza Nova. As much as he tried to enjoy his beloved cheese slices, he just looked so sick. He wasn't himself.

"It's just a cold," I kept telling myself.

This "cold" continued to play hide and seek with Emilio as he returned to school. It revealed itself again in February.

"It's just a cold."

Friends and family consoled us and said, "There is no need to worry. Colds, fevers, and coughs are normal when kids go to preschool." We didn't have any frame of reference for this reality since Emilio spent most days at home with Rosa, his nanny, from birth to age three while Richard and I worked full-time.

In March, Emilio came down with another cold and fever lasting seven days. We gave him Baby Tylenol, as Dr. Raymond Evans, Emilio's pediatrician, suggested. Within a few hours, the fever subsided. Forty-eight hours later, it came roaring back. My sister-in-law, Linda was visiting at the time and said, "Emilio looks so pale. You ought to have one of those tests done to see if he's anemic."

Within a few days, nothing was normal about what was happening to Emilio. Red flags started flying when we noticed bruises the size of a dime develop on his arms and legs. He looked pale and sick, and his behavior became lethargic. When we reported this news to Dr. Evans, he firmly instructed us to come into his office immediately.

It was a Monday morning, March 27, 1998, my 45th birthday. Dr. Evans ran a series of blood tests. He assured us that he would call the following day with the results. He gently said, "Try not to worry too much. It could be a couple of different issues that are all treatable. We will do everything possible to take care of Emilio."

That evening Richard returned home with my favorite birthday cake, tiramisu. In another bag, he surprised us with a gallon of vanilla ice cream, Emilio's favorite flavor.

I prepared a chicken vegetable soup and served it with a loaf of homemade sourdough bread, a birthday gift from my neighbor Sandy. After dinner, the three of us ate my birthday cake and ice cream on the living room floor while we played with Emilio's favorite Legos.

Before bedtime, Emilio begged me to turn on one of his movies, "Beauty and the Beast." He loved the part at the end of the movie when Belle danced with the Beast. "Sing the song, Mommy!" He said this repeatedly until I picked him up, and we waltzed around the living room, as we had done so many times since he was a baby. This hauntingly beautiful song expresses the feeling of love being timeless and ageless—my sentiments exactly. My love for Emilio had no end, and it would go on forever and always.

As Emilio laid his head on my shoulder that evening, I felt the fear sweep in as it overtook my every thought.

Having put Emilio to bed, I tried desperately to fall asleep, but I couldn't rest. All I could think about was what Dr. Evans's news would be in the morning. Richard tried hard to console me, but all I could say was, "Do we need to prepare ourselves for crippling news about Emilio's health?" Richard had no words. All we could do was hold on tightly to one another and try to get some sleep. At some point in the night, I felt Emilio's tiny cold feet on my back and realized that he must have crawled into bed with us. Surprisingly, I never felt him jump in. I was grateful for even a few moments of slumber.

That morning, March 28, 1998, we received the doctor's call at 9:00 a.m. We had both cleared our morning work calendars and prepared to drive to the doctor's office anytime. Dr. Evans instructed us to come in as soon as we could. With the phone on speaker, we both declared at the same time, "Doctor, what's wrong with Emilio?" Dr. Evans quickly responded, "I prefer to discuss Emilio's results in person."

And so, that was the prelude to the day when we were told Emilio had leukemia, and all of our dreams took a nosedive as a multitude of arrows pierced our hearts. Our raft flipped over in Class V River rapids with one phone call.

I would never let Emilio witness my sadness. Never.

I prayed out loud to God and said to Richard, "How will we ever get through this? What is going to happen to Emilio?"

Chapter 2
I See You

January 6, 1995

I was profoundly and madly in love with Emilio from the first moment we met.

By the time he was three months old, we were dining out often, and he traveled everywhere with us. When we took him out into the world, we often heard people exclaim "captivating!" and "mesmerizing!" Strangers would approach our table in a restaurant, look Emilio in the eyes, and say those words.

We would nod and reply thank you, but often felt uncomfortable. We are both pretty humble people and didn't walk around saying, "Isn't our baby gorgeous!"

But the truth is he was a beautiful baby. He was born with a full head of black hair that quickly turned blond within his first year. His eyes were as black as olives, and his skin tone was creamy and fair. Both Richard and myself have dark brown hair and eyes. We both have a darker complexion and tan easily.

Emilio had a sweet, soft manner about him, yet he possessed a strong will that reminded me of my tenacious spirit. Emilio was inquisitive from a very early age. When he was as young as ten months old, I often thought he looked at me as if he knew what I was thinking. The adage "the eyes are the windows to the soul" really held true when describing Emilio's deep, dark brown eyes. I felt I was in the presence of a wise, old soul in a baby's body.

Every year on the third Saturday in December, San Diego's Balboa Park holds the "December Nights" event at the Spreckels Organ Pavilion. This annual celebration of holiday lights attracts many families because it is very child-friendly. The Spreckels Organ is the world's largest pipe organ in a fully outdoor venue. It was constructed for the 1915 Panama-California Exposition, and its acoustic powers are phenomenal. On good days, you can hear it far outside Balboa Park.

I have enjoyed the beauty of Balboa Park since 1973 when I first moved to San Diego from Los Angeles. The early twentieth-century Spanish Colonial Revival Architecture reminded me so much of The Prado Museum in Madrid. I made this move to finish my college education at San Diego State University. The year before I arrived in San Diego, when I was 19, I toured Spain, Italy, and France with my Italian language professor, Dottore Enrico Cardone, and a group of 20 young female students from UCLA.

Upon my return to Los Angeles, I spent endless hours daydreaming about finding my way back to Europe. I did return several years later when I took a break from waiting tables and my studies. I traveled with my sister Patty, our childhood friend Melanie Yurick, and our mutual best friend, Anne Heyligers. This trip occurred a few years after Patty and I moved from LA to San Diego. The four of us saved significant money from the tips that we made in a busy, successful La Jolla restaurant. San Diego became my home and I preferred it to L.A. which endorsed a much faster pace of life. Patty and I rented a small cottage across the street from La Jolla Cove. Life was good, and I felt fortunate to live at the beach; although I had to work full-time and study for my college courses, I had nothing to complain about.

Some afternoons, I drove the 20-minute drive from my home at the beach to Balboa Park, where even a quick glance at the majestic eucalyptus trees brought me peace. My reason for venturing out to the park was to study quietly in an isolated place. In between my studies, I spent time walking through the park. There were numerous visual pockets of beauty at every turn. The gardens were filled with sumptuous roses and magnolias, and the aromas that drifted in and around the space on my blanket were those of the freshly cut lawn and the tall, broad trees that sheltered people from the warm sun.

Local San Diegans and tourists rode bikes through the park, and an entourage of serious runners and casual joggers filled the sidewalks and canyon trails. Some people took breaks from work to eat lunch and nap. I enjoyed watching them rest or read their books under the shady trees. The power of sunlight can brighten the day of even those individuals who may be suffering. Balboa Park was one place that comforted me as I navigated my way through the insecure journey of my early twenties, desperate to find my way.

When someone asked me why the twenties were such a confusing time, I would say the decade is about the complicated place between college and one's life.

It was a particularly difficult time for me because I was searching desperately to find my spiritual place in the world. As a child, I profited from the example that my parents provided for me. They were kind and compassionate to others. They went without material goods so that their six children could attend Catholic school.

My mother's religious experiences were very personal and rather simple. She had several profound encounters with Jesus in her life. She prayed hard and asked him for help. She received his support and was deeply at peace in her heart and soul. My father always sought a much deeper understanding of his earthly life, an earnest search for truth. He spent his life studying the lives of the saints. His knowledge of them quickened his understanding of his soul. His spiritual growth unfolded, and he grew closer to knowing God. They were both advanced in their spiritual place in the world and within themselves.

I admired my parents tremendously, but I needed these discoveries for myself. Like many other twentysomethings, I felt stuck between a world of earthly pleasures and an agonizing desire to discover "my truth." I was always asking myself, "Who am I? What is my purpose in this world?" I needed a teacher, and like my father, I needed religious and philosophical books to satisfy my search for understanding. I didn't know then that I would find my truth in the not-so-far-away-future.

When Emilio came into my life 20 years later, I looked forward to the time when he would become a part of our Balboa Park adventures. His first Christmas was December 1995, and on that cool, brisk evening, the three of us bundled up in sweaters, grabbed Emilio's fold-up stroller, and headed out to the park. The Southern California sun was beginning to descend over the nearby Pacific Ocean. We strolled through the park's famous Rose Garden on our way to the Organ Pavilion. Settling onto our blanket, we set up our picnic dinner.

Richard and I were ready to put the day behind us and finally enjoy quality time with Emilio. As I tried to lift him out of his stroller, he resisted and pulled himself back in. He appeared warm and cozy as he sat back and put his little right thumb in his mouth. Thumb-sucking had brought Emilio comfort since he was born, and we were in no rush to dismiss this relaxing habit. The first time we put a "binky" in his mouth, he spit it out! We felt lucky that we never had to look for a lost binky to stop him from crying or pick up a dirty binky from the floor, as so many of our friends had to do.

A solo pianist began to play Erik Satie's "Trois Gymnopedies." This particular song is a gentle, dreamy yet cerebral piano exercise. Satie's beautiful songs were a significant influence on twentieth-century music. As Richard and I stood up to see the pianist play, we glanced down to look at Emilio. He was leaning in, with his arms perched on his food tray, attentively listening to the music. I could see in his eyes he was mesmerized by what he was hearing. Watching him closely, I noticed his eyes filled with tears, although Emilio did not utter a sound. His tiny lips were quivering, yet I knew it wasn't from a chill in the air. The setting sun had left a comfortable warmth under the palm tree where we sat to eat dinner.

I suspected his tears weren't because he was hungry or needed something. I knew that Satie's enigmatically beautiful music moved Emilio. I wanted to pick him up and hold him tightly, but I bent over and gently kissed his expressive and beautiful face. Emilio glanced up at me and quietly smiled with a sweet expression. In that one precious moment, I was certain that nothing I had accomplished in my life could compare to the splendid grandeur of being Emilio's mother.

Emilio got his artistic talent and his love of nature from his father. Richard is a landscape Plein air painter, which means that he paints outdoors. He doesn't paint in a studio or from a photograph. Richard travels to a location site, sets up his easel, stands in one place, and paints for hours. His locations are mostly seascapes, but he loves to paint in the mountains and the deserts of California. Richard's florals are stunning and have graced the cover of several San Diego Magazine editions over the years.

Richard's childhood was spent most often in the backyard garden with his mother, Donaciana, most often referred to as Dancy. From her, he developed a keen awareness of what plants, flowers, and vegetables needed to thrive.

Richard passed along these teachings to our son. It took Emilio a little while to realize the growth of the garden he planted would not happen overnight. Richard explained that it could take months before tomatoes appear on the vine. Within a week of helping his dad plant the tomatoes in a large pot, Emilio would dash out the back kitchen door every morning and ask Richard, "Did the tomatoes grow yet?"

"No, Emilio, not yet. They need more time," Richard said. Emilio would bow his little head and mumble the words, "Okay, Dad. I will wait a little longer."

When I first met Richard, I was attracted to him for many reasons. He was handsome and fit. When he smiled, his eyes lit up. He was rugged-looking in a young Anthony Quinn kind of way. But the more time I spent with him, the more I began to appreciate his intelligence and sensitivity. He had a calm, secure way about him. He pulled me in with his considerate behavior. Richard spoke when he had something to say and that is a quality that I admire in a person, especially a potential boyfriend. My interest peaked early in our dating days, and I listened attentively to every word he spoke. His voice was soft and gentle, yet firm and confident. I wanted to have more conversations with this gorgeous, confident man.

Emilio took his first steps when he was barely ten months old. One morning when he crawled into our bed to snuggle with me, Richard said, "I love to watch the two of you together. Did you know that you would love him so intensely?" His sweet question caught me by surprise. I replied, "No, I couldn't have imagined how much I would love him. I couldn't have known what parental love would feel like." He nodded in agreement and said, "Sometimes loving Emilio so much is frightening, but it is also so beautiful. I am grateful not to go through life without knowing this kind of love." His words brought me comfort, and I felt exactly the same way.

Richard and I had very different childhood experiences with our mothers. He often spoke about how nurturing his mother was. His sister Linda loved sharing stories with him about how often Dancy would bundle him up in a blanket, even on a warm morning. She would hold him in her arms as she watered her plants and flowers. Linda and Richard's brothers Gilbert and Charlie would say to their mother, "Mom, you are smothering your baby!" As the story goes, Dancy would just laugh and reply, "He's my last baby, and I am going to hold him for as long as I can."

After Emilio's birth, we ventured out one Sunday afternoon to introduce him to Dancy and Richard's dad, Zeferino. We wrapped Emilio up papoose-style in a blanket one of my girlfriends made for him. The blanket was colorful, with patches of open yarn weaving in and around the colors of brown and gold. As I handed Emilio over to Dancy, her first words were, "This blanket has holes in it. He must be so cold." Richard had prepared me for the fact that she might say this.

Watching my mother-in-law comfort my son was a beautiful sight to see. It was easy to understand why Richard loved us so much. He was taught by the best, his mother.

In those first few months of Emilio's life, I wanted to spend every moment with him. It was hard for me to return to work when he was just eight weeks old, but like most couples, we needed both of our incomes. My social life took a back seat because I couldn't wait to get home to Emilio at the end of my work day. Richard and I took nothing for granted, and we thanked God every day that Emilio came into our lives. We were first-time parents in our forties who finally got the chance to see the world through our child's eyes.

Together, we taught Emilio to be kind and loving to all God's creatures, and in return, he became our teacher, even in the first few years of his life.

Chapter 3
At the Core

Looking back on Emilio's childhood is sometimes like looking into a kaleidoscope, where one scene from the past shifts into another. My memories of growing up didn't include feeling that I was cherished in the way I cherished Emilio.

I had not been in a hurry to start a family of my own. I think that's because I was always searching to find my way in the world, from when I was a child and continuing throughout most of my thirties. Growing up as the eldest of six children may have made me an overachiever, but it didn't do much for my self-esteem. My siblings and I were all born within nine years. With so many little ones to take care of, Mom barely had a moment to breathe; it was hard to get her attention.

As the eldest child, I was expected to help her, but I was just a little girl who looked forward to going to school every day. Then at the end of my day, I wanted to be able to talk with my mother about the joyful moments and all of the painful ones too. I learned early on that I would have to wait for her to have time for me.

I have no memories of my life before the age of seven. I would marvel when girlfriends would tell me they remembered being in the crib, as they cried and fussed until their mothers came in to pick them up. I was stunned to hear their stories of being five years old and skipping to kindergarten, like my sister Patty always did.

I remember being silent when I was seven years old and in the first grade. I was terribly shy and every time an adult would look at me or ask me how I was doing, I would lower my head and mumble the word "fine." That was all I could manage.

One evening a customer from my dad's barber shop came to our house for a visit. My mother adored this man, and when he entered through the front door, I was standing directly in front of him. He tipped his hat and said to me, "You must be Diane. You are a very pretty young lady." Mortified, I stood in silence and could not utter a word. He bent down a bit in order to look me in the eye and said, "All you need to do is say thank you, nothing more, nothing less." I mimicked his words, and quietly said, "Thank you." He smiled and moved along to join my parents for a cocktail in the dining room. He left a lasting impression on me, and the simple words "thank you" helped me get through many social gatherings and personal encounters with strangers.

My sister Patty, was already showing signs of rebellion. As I witnessed my mom's concern about Patty's behavior, I kept to myself and didn't want to burden my parents. Instead of acting out as Patty did, I retreated.

I was a good girl. I was independent and resourceful. Sometimes my mom would say, "Thank God I don't have to worry about you, Diane." When I heard these words, I would proudly nod my head in agreement. I felt valued but primarily resentful. Her words stayed with me for a very long time. Even though I increasingly needed her motherly love, I kept quiet as the babies kept on coming.

One of my first memories of how stressful my mother's life had become was when my mom and dad told me they were having another baby—this would be my mother's fifth child. My mom spoke these words in a low voice. She was shaking from exhaustion. She had just finished nursing her fourth child, my sister Nancy. Nancy was only three months old. My mother Mary's coping skills had already reached their maximum level of full competency.

At this time, I was seven years old, Patty was six, and Michael was five. Mom had a two-year break between Michael and Nancy. My mother seemed to handle two-year intervals pretty well. When she was hit with the news of pregnancy after she had just given birth to her newest baby, her entire world crashed around her, and mom became unhinged with fear.

My mother was ready for Nancy to come into her world, but it was a completely different story with Teresa. Nancy was a perfectly happy baby, an easy birth for my mom, and the only child whom my mother was able to breastfeed successfully. Dr. Romero, who delivered the four of us, told my mom that if she breastfed Nancy, she would not get pregnant. The doctor's words were a huge relief to my mom because she spent most of her day in complete exhaustion and always said, "God never gives you more than you can handle." Well, he certainly threw her out of her comfort zone. My mom knew that four children at that time could be manageable; after all, most of her friends in our neighborhood had at least four children by the time they were in their mid-thirties.

Mom and Dad were devout Catholics. They did not believe in birth control. I may have been the only planned child since I was the oldest, and my mom was already 30 years old when she married my dad. By age 31, mom was pregnant and ready for me.

When doctor Romero told mom that she was pregnant again, three months after Nancy's birth, my mom was outraged. She cursed him because he had lied to her about not getting pregnant if she breastfed Nancy. Years later, I researched the stats on that proclamation and found that in the fifties and sixties, only two out of 100 women became pregnant while breastfeeding. So, although he might have been correct, I suspect that his superior, God-like attitude, and rather brisk bedside manner, might have been responsible for getting her so angry.

That evening, she and my dad went into their room with the door closed and their stereo blasting Frank Sinatra, unaware that the three of us older kids had our ears pressed against their bedroom door. Mom screamed at my dad for being so amorous and not at all logical about the timing of what another pregnancy might bring to our family. Her cries were chilling and reminded me of a wounded animal who was suffering all alone.

Mom opened the door to find the three of us with streams of tears rolling down our faces. We were devastated to witness our parents fighting. We had never heard them argue or raise their voices with one another. "Mommy, Daddy!" I cried out, "Please don't get a divorce!" I pleaded with them to stop fighting with one another. "We will help you with your new baby," I told them in a softer voice. My dad wrapped me in his arms and said, "Everything will be alright, Diane. Please don't worry."

From that harrowing evening forward, my mother spent the next six months until my sister Teresa's birth in a state of melancholy and despair. Several years later, I realized that the expression of what I was seeing on her face was one of fear.

As young women, and again later in life, my sister Teresa and I shared many discussions about our mother's inability to be emotionally available for the two of us. My childhood experiences were nothing compared to what my sister Teresa endured. She suffered deep trauma throughout her childhood, and most significantly while in our mother's womb. Our mother was angry and emotionally unable to connect with the new life growing within her body. When Teresa was born, my mother handed her over to my father and said to him, "You take care of her now." And so, he did.

Rocco was the nurturing father and mother that Teresa needed so desperately. Patty, Michael, and I watched over her as best we could. Nancy became her best friend in the world for the next 59 years of their lives, until Nancy suddenly left us from a dreadful illness that took her away far too soon.

Many years later, during one of our "mom" conversations, Teresa said, "do you ever think about the fact that mom may have never wanted to have daughters?" I shook my head in agreement and answered back, "yes, I think you're right, she's always more comfortable being with her boys." Teresa's statement was packed with a deeper meaning. The truth was that our mom came to motherhood with a chip on her shoulder. She told us often about how offended she was by the girls in her New York neighborhood.

The little girls who were born in America would laugh at our mother's appearance and make fun of her accent. My mother and grandmother immigrated from Italy to America when she was six years old. It was always a boy who befriended her in school. Mom didn't trust girls, which was evident when she tried to understand her four daughters. Our needs were insignificant to her. Two of us, Teresa and myself, went silent. The other two, Patty and Nancy, rebelled. As my teenage years came upon me, I wished with all my heart that I had learned how to rebel. Going silent cost me a great deal of pain as time went on. I had a hard time speaking about my needs, both personally and professionally, until enough hard knocks got me back up off my feet and into the playing field, time after time.

By the time I was 14, my youngest brother John, my mother's last child, was five years old and in kindergarten most of the day. My mother finally had some time to herself with all her children in school. This period was a turning point for the two of us; every few days, she took some time to sit with me and ask me about my day. My mom would say, "Diane, what was your favorite part of your day at school?" I was delighted by her question and was finally able to share my joys and disappointments with her. I thought for a moment, then replied, "My teacher read us excerpts from Louisa May Alcott's book, *Little Women*."

My mom asked me to tell her about the book, and she surprised me when she said, "I was never able to read this book or others like it. They didn't introduce them to us in my school, but if I had taken a book like this home from the library, my father would have been furious. I am sure that he would have told me to get to work and help my mother with dinner and caring for my sisters." She said, "My father thought reading books after school was a waste of time."

I was heartbroken for her. It was a perfect example of how painful her childhood was because of her father's anger and dismissive behavior toward her.

When my mother was six years old, she and her mother, Angelina, left their small village in Molise, Italy, and traveled by ship across the Atlantic to meet my grandfather, Dominic Lamana, in New York City. My grandparents' marriage had been arranged since they were 17 years old. There was no love there, only a situation that left them both with an unhappy future. Sensing her mother's reluctance to leave her village, my mother opposed the trip to America and declared her hatred of her father the moment she saw him standing on the dock.

After two weeks at sea, both nauseous, pale, and filled with regret, Angelina and Mary arrived on Ellis Island, New York, in 1929.

Stepping off the ship at the dock, they were greeted warmly by Dominic. Angelina pulled back from him with a scornful look, and as he tried to embrace little Mary, she hit him in the arm, spit in his face, and said, "I will never call you, my father! I hate you, and I want to go home!" My mother said he responded by slapping her face and shouting, "What a horrible, spoiled child you have become, no daughter of mine will ever speak to me like this again!"

Mary's tough and spirited nature was set in stone that day. That first day in America was the onset of an agonizing relationship with her father that would haunt her for the rest of her life.

From that *Little Women* moment on, my mother and I shared some reading time most afternoons. She loved the books I loved and became genuinely interested in my opinions. My mother actually listened to me and responded sensitively. She was kind and wise. For the first time in my life, I knew she loved me.

A lifetime of reflection about my mother has allowed me the generosity to view her from many different angles. It is easy for me now to plug into a viewfinder and witness her as a mama animal of sorts, having given birth to a litter of newborn puppies or kittens. I ask myself, "How much energy can one mother have? Does her compassion and instinct extend to each of us differently or in equal parts? Is one or two of her offspring more difficult than the others?"

I know now that she did the best she could. If some of us needed more, we got what we got. Whatever we lacked, we had our dad who was always there to fill in the gaps. And for Teresa and myself, we eventually found what we needed when we married and became mothers.

In time, I understood the blessings that come from being a part of a large family. The six of us watched out for one another and always appreciated our differences. We are a tribe, and caring for one another has become our good fortune.

My father, Rocco Cappetta, was a devoted husband and a nurturing father to his six children. At the end of his twelve-hour work day, Rocco would endure one hour of stop-and-go traffic on the 405 North freeway working his way from the westside of L.A. to our modest home in the

San Fernando Valley. By the time he would walk through the front door, the six of us kids had eaten dinner, and our mother was warming up his home-cooked meal.

The minute we saw my father, we would climb all over him until mom would swish us away as she repeated the exact words every weekday evening, "Brush your teeth and do your homework! Your dad needs to eat in peace." Mom directed him to the kitchen, then closed the door in an attempt to give him just 30 minutes of peace and quiet.

Those few moments at the kitchen table each evening were perhaps the only quiet time the two could count on. Mom had already eaten, but she poured a tiny glass of red wine for the two of them. She would then catch her breath and ask him, "How was your day, Mike?"

Rocco's middle name was Michael, and when he immigrated to America from Italy as a young boy, he adopted the name "Mike." As an immigrant fourteen-year-old in New York, he was often made fun of for not speaking English properly. Introducing himself as Mike instead of Rocco got him much farther with the local boys on the streets, along with the boxing classes he took in school.

My mom's rejection stories seemed more painful than my dad's memories. Mary came to America when she was only six years old. She was constantly teased because she was a foreigner and didn't speak English. She introduced herself as Mary, certainly not her birth name, Maria. My mom always preferred to call my dad Mike instead of Rocco.

At our kitchen table, most evenings, Mike would reply to Mary's questions by sharing a funny story or two about his customers who graced his barbershop that day. It was good to hear my mom laugh. She typically had no time to do so during her day. When my dad would ask her how her day was, she would exude a sigh and tell him that everything was okay. I was sure he intuitively knew that her passivity was her way of letting him know how utterly exhausted she was.

I knew about their evening dinner conversations with such certainty because my sister Patty and I were frequently sneaking away from our homework and mischievously listening at the kitchen door to their discussions. Upon occasion, my mom caught us.

My dad knew how to make my mom smile, and in those quiet, special moments at the kitchen table, I am confident that her sighs of despair turned to joy just being back in his presence. Her lovingly prepared meal brought him comfort and calm after his long day of serving others and listening to their stories. My mom always told us that my dad was the one who taught her how to trust others. He was her rock, and she was his blessed Mary.

Every school night, after his dinner, my dad would tuck each of us into bed. He continued to do this no matter how old we were. He would ask about our day and sit by the side of our bed until one of us had finished our stories, and then he would move on to the next child. If he didn't know the answer to one of our math or science questions, he would grab the appropriate encyclopedia from the living room bookshelf and have that answer for us the following morning before breakfast.

My dad gave me dignity at a time in my life when I was very insecure about so many aspects of myself. In my junior year of high school, my boyfriend made sure I was nominated for the Homecoming Court, which would have given me the opportunity to become Homecoming Queen if chosen. Unbeknown to him and myself, some of his football-playing buddies decided to stuff the ballot box with numerous amounts of small, yellow paper clippings with my name on them.

One of the priests, Father Brian, discovered the deceit and immediately called my boyfriend into his office. Bradley was a well-respected senior and captain of the football team in this small Catholic Highschool on Ventura Boulevard in Encino. Bradley denied knowing anything about this fiasco and quickly deferred to the other rascals who must have been responsible. He pleaded with Fr. Brian, "Please, Father, dismiss these votes and allow us to move forward with the evening game and celebration, this was just a prank from some players, and they will be remorseful, I promise!"

According to Bradley, Fr. Brian directed him to bring me to the field, as planned, at 5:00 p.m. I would meet the rest of the prom court and attend the game, and half-time procession. Nervous and unsure about how the evening would unfold, I did as I was told.

On the night of the homecoming game, I was wearing the long, white dress with lace-covered sleeves that my mother had made for me. We used almost an entire can of Aqua Net hairspray to poof up my pixie haircut and placed pink-and rose-colored flowers on top of my head. Patty did my makeup, which included a flattering dark pink shade of lipstick. I was ready to go two hours prior to arrival time.

My mother, sisters, and brother Michael were in the grandstands, ready to cheer me on when my car circled on the track in front of their seats. And there was my dad. Rocco was a man of integrity and gentleness who inspired many others throughout his life. My dad was always there for me no matter how old I was. This evening, I truly witnessed his grace and influence in my life.

As Bradley and I stood on the football field, he sheepishly told me that I had been disqualified. I knew the "ballot-stuffing" episode was a disrespectful display from the other players, but no one told me I was officially "disqualified." Despite this, Fr. Brian insisted that I ride in one of the cars designated for the homecoming court's parade.

Before I could rebel and refuse to do so, I was shuffled off to a beat-up, old black Chevy jalopy where a young student driver, whom I had never met, was waiting for me. The other four queen candidates were seated high on the back seats of bright-colored Impala convertibles; my car was the last one in the lineup. As a (former?) member of the court, I received a bouquet of white roses. Holding the bouquet, I took my place in the old convertible, sat up straight and wondered what had gone so terribly wrong.

The drive around the football field felt like a spin around one of Dante's circles of hell. When my car reached a certain point, my boyfriend and my entire family came down from their seats, their heads towering over the chained linked fence that separated the crowd from the football field and the princess cars.

"Stay strong, Diane. We are so proud of you!" they shouted. They said something about boys stuffing the ballot box with my name. "That's why you're riding in that car, at the end!" they said.

As it turned out, several of our junior and senior friends had played what was ultimately a cruel trick and stuffed the ballot box with my name. They told my boyfriend they wanted to ensure I won. Of course, I had nothing to do with it, nor did my boyfriend. It was later revealed these rascals wanted to impress my boyfriend, who was a football hero at their school.

When the cars stopped, Maryann McPherson, girlfriend of the quarterback Tommy Green, won the title of Homecoming Queen. But what mattered to me was the sight of my father briskly running in my direction. He gently put his arms around me and held me tightly as he whispered in my ear, "Oh my sweet Diane, nothing was your fault. The boys foolishly wanted to make sure you won. We are so proud of you, with your head held high, as you drove by waving to the crowd with your beautiful smile."

I knew at that moment nobody could take me down. I was proud and positive, no matter how much pain and humiliation I felt that evening. My dad's words are what stayed with me, and they helped me continue to hold my head high throughout the rest of my life, even in my most excruciating, humbling moments. Though I struggled with self-doubt, I never stopped believing I could do whatever had to be done.

A dad like Rocco was a hard act to follow for any young man who courted one of his four daughters. I spent all my twenties and the better half of my thirties looking for a man like Rocco.

Chapter 4
Challenges and Blessings

Waiting tables throughout my twenties was a carefree existence even though I was studying hard to complete my college courses. In those days, tips were abundant and easy cash in my pocket at the end of a seven-hour shift. Five evenings a week, Patty and I would walk up the hill from our La Jolla cottage and strut through the massive redwood doors of The Bratskellar Restaurant on Prospect St.

We wore flowing white peasant shirts and long, floral skirts. We tied a crisp black apron around our waists and walked straight into our six-table station, ready to relieve the day shift waitress or waiter, who couldn't wait to go home or to the bar next door by that time. We never stopped moving from the first table we approached at 5:00 p.m. until midnight.

The Bratskellar was the busiest restaurant in La Jolla, with patrons of all ages and sizes. Tourists were abundant in La Jolla all year round. San Diego's climate was most often the perfect 73-degree day, and people from all over the country, and the world, came to visit this little gem of a town with her glorious beaches, coves, and retail shops. We were blessed and happy.

Those years flew by, and by the time I approached thirty, I knew I had better give up my apron and begin focusing on a more serious career. After all, I had a college diploma and had traveled numerous times to Europe, yet I had no particular job skills beyond waiting tables. I applied for a management position in a downtown corporate restaurant chain. I learned the business from the general manager and bookkeeper and spent my training days working in every facet of the restaurant. I shadowed the line cooks, chopped lettuce with the prep cooks, learned how to run the dishwashing machines, made cocktails with the bartenders, worked the busiest nights as a bar-back, and bussed tables with the high school kids.

Three months later, I was an official assistant manager who worked six 10-hour shifts each week, with two days in a row off once a month. I worked evenings, weekends, and every holiday. I kept this grueling schedule for the first half of my precious thirties. I started waiting tables when I was fifteen to pay my tuition and stay in my Catholic girl's school through graduation. It was the late 1960s when the Vietnam War and the hippie movement began. Men and boys stopped cutting their hair. My dad's barber shop business took a nosedive, and my mom was clipping coupons to keep the eight of us fed. I did my part and stayed in school with my comfortable tribe of friends.

Besides making a good living, waitressing gave me lots of freedom and many friends. Nothing about the restaurant industry was boring. However, the demands of restaurant management were overwhelming, and my job soon became an incredible burden. For me, the restaurant business was definitely not conducive to meeting one's life partner and living a balanced personal and professional life.

It was a tough reality check, and by the time I celebrated my 36th birthday, I was still single and not dating anyone who was a candidate for a serious relationship. I had been spending a great deal of time on self-reflection and doing the work it took to become self-sufficient. A couple of my single girlfriends and I would laugh at ourselves when we spoke about the fact that we had become like "self-contained RVs." We all wanted to attract a partner who was the same way.

I was getting worried as my "biological clock" was ticking away. Frantically pondering my situation, I told Patty one day, "I am so scared that I might miss the opportunity to have a family of my own. I finally really want one." With tears in my eyes, I continued, "Perhaps I have selfishly waited too long?"

I recently found out that my mother was telling our relatives and her friends, "Diane has never been interested in dreaming about her wedding day. That is not even on her radar!" She was completely correct. What I didn't feel comfortable telling my mom was that because I grew up with so many kids around me, I never dreamt about having children either. Although I didn't have the guts to tell her, I am sure she knew.

Patty's response was one of sincere support as she said, "Diane, you were never that little girl or teenager who talked about wanting to get married. Don't be so hard on yourself. You were the oldest of six kids, and you often had to put your own needs on the back burner. You deserve to have lived your life exactly as you have, free of responsibility for others, in pursuit of reaching your dreams. You will find the right person. I just know you will!"

Patty's words were so sweet, but I knew one thing for sure, I would have to take my dating search as seriously as my career search. Since I was only meeting guys in the industry, I needed to start networking with everyone I knew outside of the restaurant business.

Of course, I had the best father, which was difficult because I always wanted to meet a man like Rocco. Also, it was no longer funny to me that perhaps because of my gypsy soul, I had forgotten to have children!

Eventually, I realized that if my life was going to change, I had to get out of the restaurant business.

I began asking my family and friends, "How can I remain in an industry that demands working on evenings, weekends, and holidays?" Nothing about the restaurant business allowed working Monday through Friday day shifts. It never happened. I repeatedly asked my girlfriends, "How will I ever meet the right man if all I do is go to work when he returns home and is ready to cook a meal together or enjoy an evening out with me?"

I soon knew something had to change the day I ended up on the bathroom floor.

It was my brother John's wedding day, May 1991. My baby brother John had met the love of his life, my sister-in-law Nancy Jo Kupiec. Nancy Jo was born and raised in Pittsburgh, Pennsylvania. Their wedding was spectacular, and our entire Cappetta family flew together from San Diego to Pittsburgh for this glorious weekend of celebration. I was the only sibling who was not married. It was particularly distressing for me because I was the eldest and John was the youngest.

I started out feeling happy and festive that weekend. However, my mood began to change when we were two hours into the late afternoon reception. Having consumed at least three glasses of champagne while I danced with John's single guy friends, all nine years my junior, I soon found myself in the ladies' room in a bathroom stall, on the floor, crying my eyes out.

Young women, older women, and an array of little girls came in and out of the bathroom as I choked back my tears. Within the following 30 minutes, my sister Patty came in, called out my name, and stuck her head under the stall where I lay shamefully uttering words of embarrassment, "Patty, I feel so ashamed of myself! How can I be so selfish, thinking about myself on this glorious day for our brother and his new wife!" Patty swooped me up, wrapped her arms around me, and calmly reminded me that I would also find the love of my life in the near future.

Within a few moments, Pia Tinsley, who had recently married John's childhood best friend, Bobby, put her arms around me and said, "Oh Diane, don't worry, you will find the love of your life! You will have a family if that is what you want. It is all waiting for you, just around the corner." Her voice was firm but loving. Pia then added the words, "You must be ready for him. Once you are, he will show up!"

A few days after I returned home from the wedding, I began my search for another career. I had to be discreet because the San Diego restaurant community is a microscopic world, and I could not risk my employers knowing that I was looking for something else. Within a short time, the world of sales in the wine industry opened up to me. Although I was serious about my search to find a proper husband, landing a career that suited marriage and family became the top priority. Better said, the two searches could co-exist.

An interesting job offer was soon on the table. I started in an entry-level position with a company called Wine Warehouse, based in LA. The year was 1990. The open position was in San Diego, selling wine to small stores. The offer was that I would transfer to a restaurant territory after one or two years because of my experience working with chefs, sommeliers, and restaurateurs.

Some days were tougher than others. Certain store owners weren't very accepting of women sales reps. One customer in particular always glared at me when I entered his store. He didn't take me seriously, and I marveled at how quickly he could get from the register to the backroom to hide whenever he saw me walk in. It took time to win his respect and eventual friendship.

It was the early nineties, and there were only a handful of women in the industry. Occasionally we would get together and share stories about the challenges we faced in the male dominated world of wine and spirits. Although we were competitive with each other, we helped one another by role-playing scenarios of the various obstacles that we could encounter as women; such as sexist attitudes, or demeaning comments about our limited wine knowledge, which most often were not true. To be fair, there were several store owners who were true gentlemen. I was honored to know them, and some of them remain my dearest friends today.

My wine tribe of saleswomen often laughed together as we mutually agreed that at the end of the day our goal was simply to write a big wine order, then get the heck out of there!

I didn't care if it took two years of schlepping cases of wine by myself into a liquor store. I had finally made my way into the wine industry. I had the opportunity to work hard by day and enjoy my life in the evenings and on the weekends. I knew that I had a lot to learn about outside sales and fine wines, but I was delighted that a reputable company gave me the chance to learn on the job.

It didn't take long, and I was suddenly presenting and selling wine to chefs and restaurant managers who cared about quality instead of just cost.

This was pre-internet; therefore, my education came from books and conversations with new friends who had been in the industry for several years. Pre-internet also meant that there were no online dating sites to meet new men. I spent my free time networking with friends and letting them know I was seriously interested in pursuing a healthy, sustainable relationship.

I spent endless hours reading Sales 101 books and practicing role-playing with my brother Michael. Michael is two years younger than me and has had a very successful sales career. After graduating from UCLA, Michael traveled south to San Diego to join Patty and me. Mike got an apartment with a couple of high school buddies and tended bar in La Jolla until he landed a sales position with Zellerbach Paper Co. Michael moved up quickly and eventually made his way into sales management with Staples Corp. He and his wife, Roberta, met when he was working at Zellerbach. Roberta worked hard in her career and always landed in the "Top 5 Salesperson" category every month.

My brother Mike became my mentor. He told me, "Working in sales is an amazing career if you are a self-motivated person. You are the only person who knows what you do during your work day, so it doesn't always work for certain people. However, if you stay engaged and motivated, you will eventually find freedom, independence, fun, and a very financially secure career." I took his words to heart. I knew that I could do this.

My wine studies were intense. Learning about the noble wine grapes of the most important wine regions in the world was incredibly intimidating in my early years. It took me hours most days to understand the difference in flavors between Cabernet Sauvignon from Bordeaux and Cabernet Sauvignon from Napa Valley. My colleagues told me that as soon as I got a restaurant territory, I would sell wine to some of the most sophisticated sommeliers in the city. They assured me that one day I would learn how to differentiate not only what the grape was but its country of origin and what vintage (year) the grapes were harvested. All of this, in a blind tasting with no labels, to look at!

In the restaurant business, I learned how to taste wine properly and educate the staff, but most often, I trusted my sales reps to lead me in the right direction when I wrote a new wine list. Now, I was that sales rep. I needed to be the expert for someone else. That was my job.

In time, my wine career enabled me to circle back to my true love of all things Italian. The wine industry gave me the opportunity to speak the necessary cordial words in

Italian and travel regularly to Italy, France, and Spain. I spent time learning from some of the most renowned winemakers in the world. I tasted Cabernet Sauvignon and Merlot in the grand chateaux of Bordeaux. On that particular work trip, my colleagues and I sipped Chateau d' Yquem Premier Grand Cru Sauterne while munching on fresh croissants as we toured this famous winery at 10:00 in the morning.

I learned that Chardonnay and Pinot Noir never tasted better than they did when I was in the region of Burgundy, France. However, today some of the very finest wines made from these two "Old World" grapes are rivaling France in the vineyards of Santa Barbara, and the Central Coast of California, the high mountain appellations of Sonoma, and the beautiful maritime vineyards of Oregon and Washington State. I loved teaching about the superior quality of the delicious grapes which grow in the Rhone Valley and the South of France. The elegant wines produced from the "New World" countries of the United States, Australia, New Zealand, South Africa, Chile, Argentina, and other countries began to rival Europe with their increased quality.

In my career, I had the chance to hang out with Italian families who owned small and big wineries in Tuscany, Piedmont, Venezia, and Southern Italy. I flew on private jets between Bordeaux and Tuscany with some of Sonoma Valley's greatest winery icons. At sunset, I walked through the vineyards of Rioja, Spain, after touring The Prado Museum and other sights in Madrid by day.

Within two years, I transitioned away from my entry-level sales position straight into the supplier side of the wine industry. It was 1992, and my career was fast-forwarding much more quickly than I ever imagined. A well-respected Italian importer hired me to cover San Diego County.

This transition is where my return to Italy really began. I fulfilled my wine education studies by receiving the Level One and Certified Level on the Court of Sommelier. Many years later, with Banfi Vintners, I achieved my CSW, Certified Specialist of Wine. Working for the Mariani family of Castello Banfi was the highlight of my career. Third-generation CEO Cristina Mariani-May became my mentor and remains one of my greatest friends to this day.

Settled into my career, I finally found where I belonged.

Now it was time to work on my personal life. I desperately wanted a family of my own. To my dismay, "my Rocco" was not in plain view.

It was the summer of 1992, and my neighbor and her husband introduced me to a potential dating prospect. His name was Robert. He was single, athletic, and in their words, "emotionally available."

Upon meeting him for coffee in a Del Mar oceanfront cafe, he immediately told me that he lived in Denver, Colorado but came back to San Diego every summer to visit his parents. He seemed nice enough and was very handsome. "I was fortunate to retire early," he explained as we munched on croissants and sipped our cappuccinos. He appeared to be in his late forties and was very fit. He continued, "I swim in the ocean most mornings when I am in San Diego, even if the water temperatures are a bit cold."

I was impressed and interested in getting to know him better.

After one month of seeing one another, it became apparent that Denver Robert may still be single because his polite manners were increasingly shifting to subtle remarks of a condescending nature. "You know," he said one morning as we hiked the Del Mar coastline, "You could really tighten up your legs if you added swimming laps to your exercise routine." Ouch, this critique of the status of my thighs was beginning to remind me of my high school boyfriend, Bradley Summerville.

Bradley visited me often at Wil Wright's Ice Cream Parlor, where I waited tables during my junior and senior years of high school. One evening, he surprised me with his words, "Gosh Diane, it looks like you might be dipping into the ice cream container a little more than you should." Subtle words that came with the impact of a bee sting. "Hey," I quickly said, in an outraged tone, "Don't ever make comments about my weight. It is none of your business." He meekly apologized and didn't mention it again until about three weeks later, when he joined me for dinner after my shift. Bradley held up an index card with the number 105 written across the middle. "Just think, Diane," he smiled and said, "This is what you could weigh if you stopped eating ice cream after work."

Needless to say, that relationship didn't last much longer. About a year after we split up, Bradley brought his fiancé in for ice cream one evening while I was working. I was furious at the hostess for seating him in my station. She knew he was my ex-boyfriend. He introduced me to Corinne Ashley, whom he would soon marry. He ordered her lemonade and a hot fudge sundae for himself. Corinne looked like she weighed about 90 lbs., on her 5'5 frame. A few minutes later, his dessert arrived.

Corinne instantly began salivating over the sight and smell of Bradley's sundae. Glancing back over my shoulder, I saw him push the sundae away from her as she attempted to steal a bite from him. While she meekly sipped her lemonade, I walked away with a sly smirk on my face, thanking God that it wasn't me in that seat.

As my new, prospective boyfriend, Robert, was beginning to parrot Bradley's words more often, I broke up with him and swore to myself that I didn't need a boyfriend! As sad as I felt, I knew I could navigate my life on my own until I was sure the next man, I cared about was able to appreciate me completely for who I am inside and out!

It became evident that marriage and family may not be in the cards for my future as that summer progressed. I had changed careers to have time to meet a good man, but I still wasn't meeting anyone I considered to be long-lasting. I was beginning to think of other ways in which I could share all the love that I had in my heart. I planned to become a "Big Sister" to a young girl in need and was looking forward to spending more time with my many nieces and nephews.

My life wasn't so bad. I had just turned 39 and finally had the career of my dreams. However, I soon discovered that God had a different plan for me.

Chapter 5
The One

I was standing on the patio of my girlfriend's restaurant with several other women, sipping champagne on a warm summer evening. He was at the inside bar with a couple of buddies, drinking a beer and staring at me with a slight grin on his handsome face. Shifting my gaze away from his, I nervously realized: Here I go again! A handsome face, a new man, another potential heartache.

My friend Laurie Woodside was the restaurant owner of 515 Fifth. It was located in the heart of what is now San Diego's renowned downtown Gaslamp District. Within moments, Laurie dashed quickly in front of me and whispered in my ear, "Are you still dating Mr. Colorado?"

"No," I answered in a firm voice.

Laurie marched me straight inside the restaurant and over to his bar stool, "You're coming with me," she said.

"Hi," he said with a smile, "My name is Richard." He appeared to be about 5'9, slim build, and definitely fit. He had wavy black hair and lovely dark brown eyes. His style was casual yet elegant. He wore a black t-shirt, jeans, and brown leather slip-on shoes.

I surprised myself at how nervous I was feeling. "Darn it," I thought. I was just beginning to give up on my search to find the man of my dreams, and here stood another handsome prospect.

Richard pulled up a seat for me and introduced me to his friends. Laurie hung around for a few minutes, ensuring I was comfortable meeting her male tribe. Richard's buddy, Kurt, quickly said, "How many women are out on the front deck and who are they?" I replied, "About ten industry friends of mine, tasting a variety of Laurie's champagnes."

"Industry friends?" Richard quickly asked me. I answered, "Yes, we all work in the wine industry, and Laurie is one of our best customers. We gather monthly to catch up with one another and share our trials and tribulations!" He laughed and said, "Wow, it sounds like a fun career. I, too, appreciate fine wine and great food." Off to a good start, I slowly began to feel more comfortable around him.

I put off a date with Richard for a couple of weeks because my fear of relationship failure got in the way. My dismal track record was still haunting me, and I only felt safe when I wasn't being distracted by a charming man.

Finally, I agreed to meet him back at Laurie's bar and asked Laurie to sit down with me as a safety net. Overwhelmed with work, she lasted only a few minutes, soon excusing herself to get back to her guests. Almost immediately, I felt safe to slip into a beautiful, unbound place with Richard, and she could tell.

Richard lived across the street from 515 Fifth in a big, airy loft. He would spend hours painting and occasionally look down at Laurie in the bar and wave. Richard and his buddies would meet to grab beers at Laurie's bar.

Richard pointed to his studio and said, "The building was built in 1925. The Spanish historical structure is all original, as are the columns and soft orange awnings."

I loved the sound of his voice. He spoke with authority, and yet there was a gentleness about him.

From the moment of this first date, Richard and I never stopped talking.

I felt so confident with him that I belted out, "Being with you is like spending time with my best friends." He replied, "How so?"

"Well," I said, "We seem to share so many similar interests: touring museums, music festivals, long walks on the beach, and mountain hikes. Food and fine wine are important to you, and exploring new restaurants and art galleries." Richard seemed incredibly relaxed as he said, "Of course, these are the pleasures of life and our budding new friendship." Hearing his words, I suspected that life with him would never be dull. I was intrigued from the start.

After two weeks into dating, I took him to meet my sister Patty, who worked in a very popular Italian restaurant Piatti at La Jolla Shores. We sat down at Patty's station and ordered a sausage pizza and two glasses of Banfi Chianti Classico Riserva. My sister, my dearest confidant, was meeting my latest romantic interest for the first time. She was skeptical at first because she too was not terribly trusting of single men in pursuing her sister's affections.

By the time we were eating our pizza and deep into another comfortable conversation, Patty stopped by the table to check on us. I knew that Richard's sweetness to her, and his obvious interest in me, were beginning to soften her. To my surprise, Patty bent down, lifted his face upward, and put both of her hands on his cheeks, patting him gently. "Oh yes," she said, "You are special. You are different." I was mortified and knew I would have to tell her later that her words were too much, too soon. But to my surprise, Richard answered her softly, "I can tell you with confidence that I am falling in love with your sister." That was it for Patty! From that moment on, she was hooked.

Richard supported himself as a picture framer in a downtown art gallery/retail shop. He was also a passionate Plein air painter. On his days off, he would go on location and paint outside: at the beach, in the mountains, in the desert, wherever he saw beauty that inspired him to create on canvas.

Richard explained he had been drawing and painting since he was five. His dream had always been to be an artist, specifically a painter. He received his BA in Fine Arts from San Diego State University (SDSU), my alma mater, in 1977 and studied fine arts at the San Francisco Art Institute. He always worked as a framer to support his true passion, painting.

Richard planned to complete his master's degree and teach art in the San Diego community college system. Unfortunately, he was a victim of Proposition 13 and found no available teaching positions in San Diego. The year was 1976, and Prop 13, California's most famous and influential ballot measure, had just won. Prop 13 reduced tax rates on homes, businesses, and farms by about 57%. This was a great thing for many people, but now the state needed to finance public schools and community colleges, therefore the funds from local taxes were diminished.

He did not want to leave California.

Richard and I had walked a similar path. I waited tables to support myself while I figured out what I wanted to do next. Richard did the same with framing, although he always knew what he wanted to do. We were both from immigrant families and were "blindly driven" in our careers. Soon into our dating, Richard told me that he was particularly comfortable with me because I also fully embraced my roots and identity.

While my parents and grandparents had immigrated to Ellis Island from small Italian villages, Richard's grandparents immigrated to San Diego from the same small village, Purepero in the state of Michoacán, Mexico. His father, Zeferino Nares was born in Santa Ana, California. He was the fourth child of seven siblings. As a boy, he and his brothers joined their father, working long hours in the fields of Orange County and San Diego.

Zeferino met Richard's mother, Donaciana Magdeleno at a church dance in Santa Ana. The two families knew one another in Purepero. Orange County and San Diego represented the land of opportunity for their parents. Dancy was born in Purepero and came to Santa Ana with her mother and father when she was two years old. She was the oldest child of eight siblings.

After their marriage and the birth of their oldest son Gilbert, Zeferino worked as a supervisor at Conrock Cement Company. He worked long, hard hours as Donaciana ran the home and cared for their children.

My parents met in 1949 at an Italian-American Church Dance in downtown Los Angeles. As the story goes, Rocco literally "swept Maria off her feet on that glorious Saturday evening." It was love at first sight for Mary and Mike and a beautiful love story for almost 50 years. With tears in her eyes, my mother would tell her six children that our dad was the person who taught her how to love and how to trust others.

My grandmother, Angelina, loved my dad as if he were her own son. She trusted him completely. She told us that the day Mary and Mike were married, she knew that now her daughter's life would truly begin.

After several dates, Richard invited me up to see his loft and his paintings. Scanning the room, I couldn't believe what I saw—an altar with photos of Eastern religious gurus alongside a photo of Jesus Christ. On a small bookshelf to the right of the pictures stood copies of the same two books that graced my home altar, the Bible and the Bhagavad Gita. I instantly discovered that we shared our religious/spiritual identities.

Richard and I were both committed to living a life of the mind and one of appreciation for art, beauty, and nature. We shared books and always enjoyed critically discussing their more profound meaning. We began speaking for hours about the fact that each of us had spent a significant part of our twenties searching for a spiritual service where we felt most comfortable.

We had both grown up in the Catholic faith. Our parents and some of our siblings were devout Catholics. Although my father lived a very "Christ-like" life, his faith was predominately based on theology and an astute study of Catholic history and dogma. My mother's spiritual life came easy for her. She was not stuck in her head about religion. She was a believer, knew Jesus, and had experienced hands-on proof that there was indeed a God.

She was devoted to believing in the power of prayer every day of her life. My mother, Mary, had witnessed miracles and shared her stories with me. She was quiet in her faith and absolutely sure of God's existence and her own destiny.

I was blessed to have experienced one of my mom's "miracles" when I was graced with the opportunity to travel to Paris with her in the spring of 1985. Our travel entourage was my mom, dad, my cousin Lynn and her mom Aunt Eleanor, my mother's sister. We started our trip in Bedford, England, visiting my mom and Aunt Eleanor's cousins. Lynn and I met their children, our cousins for the first time. We then traveled to Paris, where my brother John had been studying that year.

I first fell in love with Paris, when I visited in 1971, I was 19 years old. On this new trip I was experiencing Paris through more mature eyes and the opportunity to tour this majestic city with John. As a local, he knew the intricacies of this historic city. His mastering of the French language was impressive. We were all having an incredible time, until later that day my mom's purse was stolen by someone in a group of roving "gypsies." John had previously warned us all that these incidents could happen, and to be careful and aware of our belongings while we frequented public places. The hotel concierge explained to us that typically children or teenage girls swoop into tourist groups so quietly that no one even knows that they are present. Within seconds my mother's purse had been stolen without my mom even realizing what had happened. Whoever positioned themselves within our circle, departed just as swiftly as they arrived. In an instant, my mother's purse was gone!

Mary screamed and cried and in disbelief she shouted, "everything was in my purse, my passport, your dad's passport, our U.S. driver's licenses too!" John reported the theft to the American Embassy and handled the details of the essential documents, but first he set off on foot with rapid speed in search of the group who stole our mother's purse. I put my arms around my mom to calm her, though that was an impossible feat. She was hysterical, and so frightened. The course of the day had changed dramatically. My dad seemed to be feeling helpless. He told me later that he was a bit ashamed that he may have put mom in a compromised situation. He said, "Diane, your mother always holds up our entire world, she runs our home, she cares for six children, and she not only handles all of our personal business, but she does the books for the barbershop too!" He finished with the words, "she took responsibility for this trip, she prepared the two of us with everything we would need. She was carrying my passport too, not only her own, I know how much she is suffering, feeling responsible, thinking she let us all down!" I said, "tell her this later, daddy, right now, you both need some rest." Returning to the hotel could not come quick enough for my mom. She was exhausted, in the thick of grief, and feeling huge amounts of remorse.

We returned to our hotel to rest before dinner. There would be no more fun or adventure for mom that day. Mom and dad returned to the room after dinner, as the rest of us went out and tried to enjoy an evening in Paris. Around 10:00 p.m. I returned to the hotel room that I shared with my mom and dad. It was a large room with three twin beds. Dad was sleeping and mom was sitting straight up in her bed with her prayer book on top of the blanket and dad's rosary beads in her hands. She said, "I want to go home Diane, my carelessness has ruined the trip for everyone."

"No mom," I said. "That is not true, these situations happen all the time, it is not your fault, we will find your purse, please get some sleep." I was so exhausted that I couldn't even wash my face. I changed into my pajamas and slipped into my tiny European bed. That night my dad and I woke often, and each time we found mom praying quietly and gently to her favorite saint.

St. Anthony of Padua was the patron saint of lost or stolen items. He was a Franciscan Friar who was canonized in 1232. Mom prayed incessantly deep into the night. She asked St. Anthony to please return her purse in the morning. She said, "I don't care about the money, or whatever else is in there, just rescue our passports and any other documents, that is all I need." She fell asleep at some point around 5:00 a.m. and finally, so too, did we.

At 7:30 a.m. there was a firm knock on the door. A woman's voice said, "Madame Cappetta, we have your purse, it was returned late last night, someone threw it inside the foyer, then ran away!" I jumped out of bed and opened the door. The director de d'hôtel introduced herself and informed us that the only thing missing from the report we had made was the American dollars, my mother's red lipstick, and her powder compact. As we suspected it was most likely a young woman or girl. The two passports and driver licenses were intact.

My mother was elated! She embraced the woman and held her tightly for a moment. The director blushed and appeared to be a bit uncomfortable. We thanked her graciously, and as she departed, my mother started to cry, and with her voice shaking, she proclaimed, "My god and my patron saint, Anthony of Padua, did not let me down, my prayers have been answered, it is a miracle!" She continued, "Let's wash up and head downstairs for coffee and those amazing French croissants!"

She proclaimed her love of Paris, and her gratitude for the divine intervention that once again proved to her that God did exist.

I was always looking for a quiet place to worship. I was happiest when outdoors in a garden or overlooking the sea. It was easy for me to meditate and quiet my mind. I believed deeply in God, a higher power. But I also believed that God was within me. God was stillness. God was goodness and compassion. I had always strived to live a life of respect for other people and all of God's creatures.

When I was seeking to find my "quiet place" to worship in my new home, San Diego, Richard was living in San Francisco, struggling as a young Catholic man to understand why the priest's sermons were condemning the gay community. Richard asked his fellow devout Catholic friends, "Isn't the church supposed to show compassion for everyone?" He would add, "Isn't that what living a 'Christ-like' life is all about?"

His search for answers brought him to other Christian services, but eventually, as I had done, he too happily landed in a place of worship that he could call his own. Like my mom, we were both committed to our own personal experiences with God. By 1980 and in entirely different cities in California, we were both identifying as Christians who embraced other world religions. After finding one another later in life, we stepped into our relationship with a solid and secure spiritual foundation.

Each of us believed there are different paths to get to God. Individually we were both finding the spiritual place where we wanted to be. We had been doing this solo for twenty years before meeting one another, and now we were on our spiritual paths together. Our yoga and meditation daily practice brought us the quiet stillness that we needed to be happy in the noisy, busy world. We soon found ourselves patiently waiting for each new day which brought us further love and joy. We cherished every moment that we spent together. We both ended up in tears as we mutually expressed how we prayed to find one another.

One day in Richard's early college years, his father told him that if he studied to become an architect, he would support him through school, but only if he was willing to give up painting and dedicate himself to architecture. Richard thanked his father but explained that he would become a painter and understood that he would always have to support himself while working hard to show and sell his paintings. Richard was committed to living his dream the way he wanted to live it.

Neither of us ever expected that someone else would make our dreams come true. We both developed serious work ethics and determined spirits at a young age. As single, nearly forty-year-olds, we lived a 24/7 work culture. Now that we had met one another, we knew it was time to find some balance. Each one of us was ready to change our lives. We had found the partner whom together, we could move through life with grace and dignity.

I fell in love with Richard for many reasons, but the fact he was a talented artist excited me. His talent for style and design intrigued me, as did his love of nature. He had a way of making me feel beautiful whenever I was with him.

Growing up in Los Angeles was challenging as a little girl and a teenager. Everyone cared so much about people's physical appearance. So many girls I knew had eating disorders, and most of us were incredibly insecure about how we looked. The other kids teased me because I looked so "foreign." I was short, with olive-colored skin, thick black eyebrows, and a prominent Italian nose. Patty got my mom's angular Roman nose. I got Rocco's rather wide one. I wore a pixie haircut throughout grade school since my dad was a barber. The look of choice in the late sixties was blonde hair and blue eyes. Green eyes worked too, but it was very important to have blonde hair if you wanted to attract a boyfriend. So, when Richard appreciated my "look," which included my bit of a round Italian body, I was grateful that this sensitive man was truly seeing me, not only on the outside but on the inside too.

After Richard met my mom and dad, he later told me that his first impression of them was his turning point. He knew then that he wanted to marry me. My parents' kindness, generosity, and love of family were exactly like his parents. Our humble beginnings stayed with us forever, and we both appreciated one another's cross-cultural experiences.

One month after our first date, Richard told me he had no plans to date anyone else. He understood that I couldn't quite yet say this to him. He followed this statement by saying, "I will wait for a while for you to be certain, but not too long." He explained that at 39 if he hadn't met the right person to marry, he would join a monastery and become a monk. A monastic life of service to God and others was a life that he had always wanted to live.

When Richard explored the various religious monasteries in San Diego, he was told that he would have until his 40th birthday to join. After that age, it would be too late. He explained how difficult it would be for him to tell his mother this news. He knew his father would understand, but his mother would be heartbroken to hear that her baby, her precious son, wanted to join an Eastern religious monastery. He knew that she would think he was joining a cult!

"Diane, I am falling in love with you," Richard said. "I suspect I may never need to disappoint my mother if you feel the same way about me. If not, I will find the words to explain my plans to my mother."

The thought of Richard joining a monastery was amazing to me. I knew how extraordinarily spiritual he was. I marveled at his ability to meditate deeply without the distraction I and many others experienced. But this kind of commitment from him was on a larger scale than a marriage proposal. Hearing his plans, I knew what I wanted to do. I took another month to reflect on my life before deciding to stop dating anyone else. Truthfully, I wasn't dating anyone else, but of course, I kept that a secret in an attempt to avoid another heartache.

I respected his confidence as I examined my resistance to making this huge commitment. But one day, just a few months after our first date, I knew he was the one. I knew that I had found my Rocco.

I fell hard. Gratefully, so did he.

Chapter 6
Family Approval

Apart from earning Patty's approval, my brother Michael's endorsement was very important to me. He was the one who introduced me to a career in sales. Once I had happily settled into the wine industry, Michael and I started chatting about my personal life. I suspected that all five of my siblings, along with my mom and dad had been chatting for years about my life. All my siblings were married with children, and I was certain that each wanted to ask me if I had any plans to give them a niece or nephew or, at the very least, a new brother-in-law.

Although he was younger, Mike had always seemed like an older brother to me. He was tall, dark, and handsome, like a movie star. Mike would have made an excellent social worker, psychologist, or life coach. He always had words of wisdom and tons of patience with his sisters. Mike was a good listener and didn't seem to mind when we would come crying to him because somebody hurt our feelings by calling us names or breaking our hearts! He was a sweet boy stuck between two older sisters and two younger sisters. This could have really messed a guy up, but not Michael. He learned how to toughen up from our dad, but like myself, he had our dad's nature. He was easygoing but hard-working.

When the four of us silly girls would hang all over our dad and dance with him in the living room on a Saturday evening, Mike could be found in the kitchen with mom, prepping food for dinner.

My brother was conscientious from a young age. He knew that once again, mom was laboring in the hot kitchen so the eight of us could be fed, and since the four girls were nowhere to be found to help her, Mike would graciously and lovingly step in. He knew that was the right thing to do.

Michael became my sounding board throughout my life. I have happily shared with him my exciting stories and my darkest and most devastating moments. When we chatted about our futures neither of us could have known what was ahead for me, for all of us. I always knew that no matter what happened, Michael would be there to pick up the phone and calm my troubled heart.

"Diane, promise me that before you get too involved with another guy, bring him to our house and let me meet him," Michael told me before I met Richard.

I welcomed his comment. I was so tired of choosing the wrong guy.

Richard and I had been dating for two months when I called Michael and said, "Hey, you remember that dinner you promised me the next time I got involved with someone?" He quickly answered, "Yes, when do you want to come over?" I knew that he had been waiting for my call. Patty spilled the beans and told him she thought I might have found my Rocco!

Roberta prepared her famous lasagna recipe that everyone adored. The two of them were so sweet and made Richard feel at home. As usual, Richard was calm and not the least bit nervous about meeting my brother. At the end of our visit, Michael gave me a high-five, and I saw in his eyes what I knew immediately when I met Richard. Michael phoned me early the next morning and said, "Diane, I think you found him. The person we met last evening is kind and sensitive, and he clearly adores you. You have my blessing."

I was delighted; my "consigliere" approved.

There was just one more profound topic to discuss…I had absolutely no idea how Richard would react to the discussion of bringing a baby into our world. One evening I casually said to him, "Maybe we should try to have a baby if it is not too late for me?"

I was surprised when he quickly replied in his usual calm voice, "Well then, let's try to have a baby."

By Christmas Eve 1992, Richard and I knew we would marry one another. When it became clear to Dancy that her youngest son had met his bride-to-be, she said to me one day, "Take care of my baby." Knowing this enormous responsibility, I willingly took it on and said to her, "I promise you that I always will!"

Richard's mother told me later that her youngest son often said, "I never want to get married, buy a house, or have children." I knew these words because I said them often to my mom and anyone who asked me, "When are you going to settle down and get married?" We set our wedding date within a few months of meeting one another. I moved into his loft, and we began our life journey together.

Chapter 7
Wedded Bliss

June 19, 1993

"They each cherish the other as a totally incredible gift from God every single day of their lives. If you know them well, then you know that this is how they treat each other. This is how they love each other."

My brother John Cappetta, at our wedding.

Our wedding was small, just family and a few close friends. We gathered in the oceanfront living room and deck of Richard's brother Gilbert's home in Oceanside, California. Gilbert, a Judge on the Court of Appeals, officiated our wedding ceremony.

My talented friend Julie Cantor, who was an excellent chef, prepared the meal. We dined on fresh baked salmon with a light layer of Julie's famous beurre blanc sauce, which was served with fresh roasted vegetables and rosemary potatoes. My other long-time girlfriend Marti Lee took the photographs and baked our gorgeous, sumptuous chocolate/strawberry crème cake. Winery associates provided French champagne and stunning white and red burgundies from small négociants in France. I wore a cream-colored suit with an elegant Christian Dior camisole underneath the jacket. The suit skirt was knee-length.

As I stood in front of the first row where my family was seated, it was my turn to recite my vows to Richard. I suddenly realized that my legs were shaking uncontrollably. For a moment, I was horrified that perhaps our guests could see my legs moving out of control! I thought to myself, how could this be happening? Gratefully, within seconds I felt a warm hand holding onto my right leg, and suddenly my shaking stopped. I calmly started to breathe again, and I noticed that my mother had grabbed onto my leg and was holding it still until I became steady and firmly grounded.

How I loved her in those moments and so many others to come.

After my "leg-shaking" experience, I advised new brides that I knew, to think seriously about wearing a long dress or a pair of elegant slacks. I had no idea I would become so nervous on my wedding day. After all, I was no longer a young, naïve girl—I clearly knew what I was doing. Throughout the ceremony, Richard was calm and focused. He told me later that evening, "I was so relaxed standing next to you in front of our loved ones. I finally knew in those moments that all of my dreams, since meeting you, were finally coming true."

In the first six months of marriage, we sold 13 paintings. It was 1993, and people were buying art. It was an exciting opportunity to add some additional income to our first year as a married couple. We took some of this income and drove up the coast to Big Sur and Carmel.

It was our first trip to two places we had both traveled to in our youth. This trip gave me insight into how incredibly focused and disciplined Richard was as a professional artist.

One morning we shopped in a small grocery stand in the heart of the Big Sur Redwood trees. We bought turkey sandwiches, chips, and two bottled waters, then headed out to scout for the perfect seascape location for Richard's newest Big Sur painting. A few miles up and down the narrow coastline, heading south from Carmel to Big Sur, Richard spotted his place.

I pulled the car over to the side of the road. He examined the space he needed to set up his easel where he would have enough room to move around. The space was very narrow and the waves crashed high within the receding tide, which was optimal for the vista point that he was seeking.

I naively asked, "Do you want me to swing by and pick you up in an hour or two?"

Assuredly, he responded, "Make it six hours from now."

What! I couldn't comprehend that he would stand on the side of the road for six hours, painting in partial fog, occasional sunlight, with waves crashing forcefully below him. All this, and cars speeding by in a lane so narrow that if they missed the turn, he could have been taken out in an instant! I couldn't have known then that his control over his fear would be the first of many times I would witness this kind of character strength that he would display in the years ahead.

I reminded him to eat his sandwich and drink plenty of water and that I would pick him up in six hours. He nodded and went immediately into that space in his head, a space that I would come to know well. In an instant, he was gone, and he heard nothing more of what I mumbled.

I took a hike at Pfeiffer State Park, enjoyed a picnic by the river, napped, and read. It was a perfect late morning and early afternoon for me. Before I knew it, it was 3:00 p.m. and time to pick up Richard.

As quickly as the morning fog lifted, the afternoon sun set in, and it became easy for me to find Richard amongst the majestic redwood trees and the glorious crystal clear, turquoise-blue water of the Pacific Ocean.

Watching him put the finishing touches on his stunning new seascape, I noticed that he had not opened his lunch bag or bottle of water. Horrified, I said, "Really? You didn't eat or sip any water?"

That's how it rolls for Richard Nares when he is painting a masterpiece. I was not only inspired by his discipline, but I was also impressed. Although, admittedly, nothing would have stopped me from eating my lunch.

Big Sur became a retreat destination for the two of us. It would take us another two years before we could return, but that second trip would be the most majestic visit of all because our son Emilio was with us.

Chapter 8
And Then There Were Three

Two months after returning from our 1993 trip to Big Sur, we were delighted to find out that I was pregnant. Almost immediately, we told our family and closest friends. This was our ultimate dream after finally finding one another, and now we would actually have the chance to know the love of having a child. The two of us were over the moon with joy.

You would think that at 40 years old, one of us would have known that it is best not to announce a pregnancy until at least 12 weeks.

Bending over with intense cramping, I made my way to the bathroom down the hallway. I felt the blood trickling down my legs as I rushed frantically to sit on the toilet seat. My pain quickly intensified. Hunching over, I laid my head on my lap, and then I soon saw what had happened. With blood filling up the toilet, I saw it. "It" was so very tiny, just a minuscule, fleshy substance. I was staring at the start of life, a life that was not meant to be—a life that could have been my baby.

I was in the house alone that morning. Richard went out for a run. It was Thanksgiving Day and we would soon be getting ready to leave for Linda's house to celebrate. I began to weep, first of all, quietly and then suddenly, in an outraged fashion. I began to shout, "How dare I think that the gift of motherhood is just going to happen so easily? I waited too long. I have been so selfish!" Once again, I returned to blaming myself and my constant obsession with being selfish. It wasn't that I was a selfish person. It was that my dreams were different from most young women's dreams at that time. Sometimes, my mother and others saw me as selfish; therefore, I internalized their comments and was certain I was.

Although I felt deep grief for my loss, I could not escape these feelings of blame. I blamed myself for my miscarriage. I was ashamed that I had spent so many child-bearing years not caring about becoming a mother. By choosing my career over motherhood, I was at risk of never knowing the greatest love of all, a mother's love for her child.

Still sitting on the toilet seat, I heard Richard enter the house from the backyard. "Richard," I shouted, "I lost our baby. Our baby died inside of me!"

I continued sobbing until he bent over and lifted me into his arms. His face was gray and shallow. He helped me clean up, then got me into bed. In an almost inaudible voice, he quietly said, "I don't have the words to speak. My heart hurts so much, Diane. I am so sorry. I am not disappointed in you or myself. I am simply speechless that this loss has occurred." He turned away briefly, then looked me in the eyes and told me, "We will try again. This must be a common occurrence for older parents. We will try again."

A few hours later, we phoned our families to tell them what had happened and to decline our visit for the day.

Neither of us felt up to joining everyone in celebrating this holiday that signifies gratitude. That morning we felt nothing to be grateful for except one another.

My doctor's orders were to lay low and try again in a few months. My clock was ticking, but I took his words seriously and eased up on my workload. I didn't want to take any risks, so I started cooking healthier meals and was grateful that I had already removed caffeine and alcohol from my life the previous year. I continued my yoga and meditation practice to lessen my ongoing stress and seriously worked on my insecurity issues about blame, guilt, and selfishness. Richard and I took long walks together, staying positive and hopeful that a pregnancy would happen again and that I could carry a baby to term.

Within a few months of our loss, I found myself pregnant again. Almost immediately, I was nauseous all day and every night. My doctor informed me that this was a very good sign. He explained that a solid pregnancy was most likely happening within my body.

My doctor joyfully told us that I was carrying twins in my ninth week of pregnancy.

I was scared to death at this news. I blurted out to Richard and my doctor, "How in the world can I work full-time and carry twins at 41 years old!"

Richard was elated by this news. The thought of having two babies, a ready-made family, was a glorious feeling to him. He assured me that he would be there every step of the way to make sure we both could work and care for our babies.

I knew that he would take on whatever needed to get done, but still, I was so very scared. I didn't know what it was like to not give 100% or more to my job. I didn't realize it at the time, but I later figured out work had always been my addiction. It was something that I needed to feel valued, worthy, and accepted. Working above and beyond what was expected of me was in my DNA.

I could picture caring for one baby, but the thought of two terrified me. My extreme fear really had more to do about my age than my job performance. Nursing, working, and limited sleep was acceptable to me with one baby, but certainly not two.

Never in my wildest dreams could I imagine caring for twins!

In my eleventh week, I lost one of my twins. I was devastated and fearful, primarily because of what might come to follow with my one seemingly healthy baby. My daily mantra became, "Oh God, please keep my baby safe. I am asking for so little, just one healthy baby!"

Richard was crushed at losing one of our babies. He was sad for several weeks. I found confidence in my doctor's assuring words that our other baby, whom we named Emilio, was thriving within me. He was developing beautifully, and we looked forward to our due date of January 22, 1995.

We both loved the name Emilio because it was a strong name that didn't need a middle name. It was the name of Richard's maternal grandfather and my mother's cousin from her Italian village.

On the first day of my last trimester, while Richard and I were driving to my weekly doctor's appointment, a very elderly man lost control of his car and slipped out of a parking lot, directly into the passenger side of our vehicle, where I was seated. Richard slammed on the brakes as the older man's car rammed through the door. I was shaken up, and as I lovingly cradled the baby inside of me, I cried out to Richard, "Please let nothing happen to my baby! The older man in the car was remorseful and appeared confused about what had just occurred.

I remember Richard shouting, 'My wife is pregnant. We need to get her to her doctor immediately!' Since we were just one block away from the medical center, a nearby ambulance saw the commotion pulled up, and swept me away to the clinic's front door, where my 'high risk' obstetrician was waiting for me.

Because of my age, I was labeled a 'high-risk' pregnancy from day one. Dr. Robert Clemens, MD, Ph.D., was a member of a special team of doctors at San Diego Children's Specialists/San Diego Perinatal Center. After an examination, he determined that my baby was fine and that I was fine but concluded that the best course of action for me was to go on bed rest for my last three months. 'Diane,' he said in a concerned voice, 'Your amniotic fluid has been reducing gradually in the past two weeks, so I am concerned for you and your baby.' Bed rest will keep Emilio safe until his due date or shortly before that."

I was so relieved. I could finally rest and concentrate on the health of my baby boy and myself. I spent the following three weeks glued to my TV watching OJ Simpson's escape as he traveled in the white Bronco through the streets of L.A. after the suspected murder of his wife Nicole and her friend, Ron Goldman. It was mesmerizing, and I was happy because I was finally safe.

Richard and I were more than ready for our next life chapter to begin. Richard completed a Winnie the Pooh painting for Emilio's nursery with Pooh and his sweet little friends. The inscription at the bottom read, "To my son, I love you very much, Dad. December 25, 1994."

We didn't buy one another Christmas gifts that year. Our greatest gift of all was arriving in just a few weeks.

Friday afternoon, January 4, 1995, was two weeks before Emilio's due date. My amniotic fluids had diminished even further. My doctor was very kind, but as my pregnancy became more complicated, his tone became more serious, and he took great caution with every day that passed.

On the day of Emilio's birth, January 6, around 3:00 p.m., Dr. Clemens nervously explained that he needed to induce labor for the baby's safety.

That familiar feeling of fear crept back into my mind. I quickly pushed this fear away and tried to remember that everything was different now; Emilio was thriving inside me. God would never let me suffer again, as I had suffered this past year in my attempts at motherhood.

I remember feeling short contractions as the epidural set in. Foggy-minded and sleepy, I heard Dr. Clemens say, "Mr. and Mrs. Nares, we are going to deliver Emilio by Cesarean; he simply does not want to join us today."

When I opened my eyes what seemed to be a short while later, Richard was gently settling Emilio into my arms. Speechless and groggy from the drugs, I was overjoyed to finally hold my baby in my arms! Nothing could have prepared me for the intense level of love that I felt for Emilio at that moment. I don't remember ever hearing my brothers and sisters, who had children before me, speak about this experience, or perhaps they did, and I wasn't paying attention.

As I held Emilio closely, Richard shared how he felt when the nurse put Emilio in his arms. He said, "Everything about the way I knew my life to be changed at that moment. Caring for Emilio is my life's purpose. My paintings are now just a small part of my life." Staring into Emilio's eyes, I knew exactly what Richard was saying. As divine intervention was responsible for the two of us finding one another later in life, so too was this ultimate gift, the birth of our son, Emilio.

When it was clearly time for Richard to return home for the night, he gently kissed Emilio's little forehead, kissed me sweetly, and told us that he would be back early the next morning. A few moments after he left our bedside, he raced back in, clearly out of breath. He told me that once he got to the parking lot, he remembered that our hospital room was directly in front of a backdoor emergency exit. He felt a surge of panic as he realized someone could come into the room and steal Emilio! I assured him that Emilio was safe, and within a few moments, he left the two of us for some much-needed sleep.

When Emilio's eyes opened gently for the first time, I said to him, "Hey little one. It's your mama!" He stared back at me, and I was startled by his gaze. He clearly knew who I was. Nine months of talking to him, singing to him, touching him through my skin, I felt as if we were rediscovering one another in a different realm of being. It was a tender reunion.

His deep, dark brown eyes never left mine until a nurse quietly said, "Hey, Mom, will it be breast or bottle?"

Exhausted and still very drowsy, I replied, "Breast." Girlfriends had told me breastfeeding was best for babies, but others informed me that it came with its own set of challenges. Like everything else in my life, I was determined to at least give it my best shot. I was not terribly surprised to hear Richard say, "I will help you make this happen if this is what is best for our son."

Chapter 9
Our Little Fighter

Since Emilio was born two weeks early, he was small and weighed 6 lbs. 2 oz.

While on bed rest, I read everything I could get my hands on about the benefits of breastfeeding one's baby. Emilio's little mouth was tiny, and it was difficult for him to latch on to me.

I would not leave the hospital until I found a solution that would enable us to try to breastfeed Emilio at home. Our exit nurse, Olivia, told us that there is a way we can feed Emilio until he grows a bit stronger and can latch on properly. She brought over a small medicine cup with a dropper. She confidently said, "Mr. and Mrs. Nares, you can put pumped breast milk into this cup and use the dropper to feed Emilio." I was mystified and said, "Like feeding a baby bird?"

"Yes," she answered quickly, "Exactly."

We knew this would be a lot of work, but we trusted her, and in a few days, Emilio was voraciously gulping down my milk from the dropper in the medicine cup. This daunting situation worked out because of Richard. He was open and willing to do anything in Emilio's best interest.

Our routine was that in the middle of the night, when Emilio needed feeding, Richard would get the pumped breast milk out of the fridge, warm it up and pour it into the medicine cup. He would feed Emilio from the dropper as I held him and rocked him back to sleep. My breasts would become engorged, and I would get up and pump to find comfort and hopefully return to sleep. Emilio often slept for the next 3–4 hours until he would awaken crying and starving for more milk.

We soldiered on, and Emilio weighed in three pounds heavier by day seven. He latched onto me perfectly and nursed voraciously. He just needed to get a little bigger, and I needed to learn how to relax. The three of us were tenacious. Gratefully our plan was successful. Despite our sheer exhaustion, we applauded our attempts to give Emilio the best start he could get. We sent a thank you note to Olivia on Emilio's eighth day in the world.

I went back to work when Emilio was eight weeks old. I took my pump on the road with me. I pumped breast milk and stored it safely throughout the day. I sat in my car or went into my customer's restroom to pump. The backseat of my car was packed with a large cooler filled with ice for the baggies of breast milk and my bottles of white wine that I was presenting to customers on my account calls.

Being a breastfeeding working mama meant I needed to continue to pump and freeze my milk so that both Richard and Rosa, our nanny, could feed Emilio. We hoped Emilio would accept the bottle. With lots of practice, fortunately, he adapted and was able to drink pumped breast milk from a bottle while I was away. He put on weight every week that passed.

I was always exhausted, but I managed to get through the work day and return home to my baby and our bonding time. I was elated and in constant awe as I watched my baby grow stronger every day.

Pumping milk, freezing it, feeding Emilio, and preparing bottles was a team effort. Apart from Emilio's birth, our introduction to Rosa Leal was our next finest gift.

Rosa lived with her family in Tijuana, Mexico. She and her mother-in-law, Toya, came to work every day in San Diego and returned home at the end of the day. Together, they cleaned the homes of busy San Diegans. We were searching for a nanny to care for Emilio while at work and a friend whom we trusted recommended Rosa.

When Rosa met two-week-old Emilio, she told Toya in Spanish, "I want to take care of this baby!" Her English was very limited, as was my Spanish, but I knew in my heart that she was a good person. Toya told us that Rosa was a kind, sensitive mother who was firm when she needed to be but loving and nurturing in a natural, sensitive way.

Rosa was very quiet and respectful. She did not have to work outside her home when her two children were born. Her loving husband Eduardo worked hard so that Rosa could stay home and care for their son Lalo and daughter Rosita. When it was time for both children to start school, Rosa felt it was right for her to earn a little income and help her husband. Rosa intended to clean a few houses with Toya a couple of days a week.

A few years into being our nanny, Rosa told us when she met Emilio, Richard, and me, she knew that we really needed her, and she knew, without a doubt, she was meant to care for this beautiful little boy. How could she ever have known what a gift she would be to the three of us.

Chapter 10
A Divine Friendship

Emilio's first year of life raced like a sprinter on the field with an unending finish line. I found myself smiling contentedly every time I watched Richard put Emilio into our Baby Bjorn Carrier, the gift we used the most. During Emilio's first six months, Richard liked to use it as a front pack so that he could feel Emilio resting on his chest. They would take long walks as Emilio slept securely fastened to his daddy's body.

As a nursing mom in Emilio's first year of life, our bonding grew and prepared the two of us for a deep connection that continued to grow. The bigger Emilio became, he was soon able to fit into the baby backpack that Richard used to continue carrying Emilio close to him. Emilio's smiles would break into laughter as he put his hands on Richard's face while Richard transitioned into a slow jog or a skip through the park.

One of the most powerful Rosa and Emilio stories happened when he was two. I was packing his little "Toy Story" suitcase for our summer vacation to Napa Valley. A winemaker and his family offered us their guesthouse in the vineyards. Emilio was so excited about our airplane ride and swimming in the pool on his daddy's back!

He was sitting on the floor in his bedroom, playing with some toys, and as I walked in, I saw that he had his little head in his lap. I lifted him up and said, "Emilio, what's wrong?" With tears in his eyes, he replied, "Mommy, I am sad that I will not see my Tia Rosa!" He opened his fist and showed me a small, multi-colored bracelet. "Tia made this for me and told me that every time I wore it, I would know that she was thinking of me."

I assured him that we would have so much fun and the time would go by so quickly, then he would be back home with Tia. He gently smiled and nodded his head. I learned a lot about Emilio that day. It was another example of his sensitivity and his capacity to love.

As a two-year-old, Emilio was filled with energy but in a calm and focused way. We kept waiting for him to crawl, but he surprised us by completely bypassing crawling, taking his first steps at ten months old. He was determined even then to get up and start moving—an intrepid explorer.

We found ourselves exhausted by the end of each day as first-time parents in our early forties. Emilio was typically asleep in his own bed by 8:00 p.m. At some point in the middle of the night, he would crawl into bed with us, and together we would all sleep until about 5:30 in the morning. Each new day would begin with Emilio waking us up with a giggle and smile. When he started speaking, one of his first complete sentences was, "Mommy, it's time for coffee!"

Emilio loved to repeat the words that Richard and I would speak to one another, such as, "Hey Diane, do you want a cappuccino or just a regular cup of coffee?"

Early morning hours brought us together on the couch as we watched PBS TV children's shows. It was 1997, and his favorite shows were: "Big Comfy Couch," "Tiny, Tom & Tilly," and "Thomas the Train."

Emilio's favorite breakfast was oatmeal and fresh fruit. He rarely ate sweets, even at birthday parties. In the evening, he would pull up his tiny stool and place it close to the stove while I prepared dinner. He loved to help me decorate pasta or rice with sauces, herbs, and spices.

We lived a few blocks from a lovely park called Pioneer in Mission Hills, a suburb of San Diego County. Emilio loved to play on the slides and swings. We put him in the stroller and walked over on the weekends.

Rosa gave Emilio another special gift. Emilio spent so much time with Rosa that he soon became fluent in Spanish. I marveled at how he so graciously switched back and forth between English and Spanish.

When Emilio was a baby, I struggled emotionally with leaving him when I had to go to work. Although I was grateful to have Rosa in our lives, my ego sometimes got the best of me as I witnessed how close they were becoming. Back then, I actually worried he might think of Rosa as his mother rather than me. Once I said to Richard, "What if Emilio loves Rosa more than me?" Richard shook his head, turned around, and walked away. "You're right," I mumbled, "That was a pretty silly thing to say."

Rosa was intuitive and must have sensed my concern. At the end of every day, when I returned home, she would put Emilio in my arms and joyfully tell him, "Momma's home Emilio!" She continued to remind Emilio of his mother's love, every chance she had in those first 12 months of his life. I have forever been grateful to her for perfectly understanding my many insecure moments. Even though we didn't even speak the same language, she just knew.

When Emilio was three, Rosa shared a memory with me. With our dictionaries in hand, she said, "My favorite memory of Emilio took place in a garden on a day we brought along a Polaroid camera. We took a picture together. I saw it and didn't like how I looked, but Emilio really liked the photo." He put it in his room, despite my protesting, saying, "Oh no, look at me, I'm ugly!"

She continued, "One day, I swapped out the picture with a photo I thought was better and tore the Polaroid up. I didn't think Emilio would notice. That hurts me so much now, still to this day, because Emilio loved that picture. He didn't see me as ugly with no make-up. He saw me as I was to him with unconditional love. I was so happy watching Emilio grow and play those first few years."

Within a few moments of sharing this story, Rosa smiled and told me she had another story to tell. "One afternoon, Emilio and I were returning home from the park to have lunch. He noticed a piece of paper under the front door. 'Leer Tia! Leer!' Translated, this means, 'Read Tia! Read!'" Rosa continued, "I told him it was an advertisement for a nanny/housekeeper who needed a job. Emilio was furious! He grabbed it out of my hand, crumpled it up with his own hands, and threw it in the trash. No, Tia, nobody else can come here, only you!" Rosa recounted.

I loved hearing Rosa's stories about how she spent her days with Emilio. They were testimonies of what we were already discovering about our little boy. Emilio was developing a strong will and mind of his own.

Most weekends, our family and close friends invited us over for meals and playtime. They were so happy that Richard and I could finally experience the precious moments that having a child can bring. They all loved him and were in awe of how we nurtured Emilio. They knew us when we only had ourselves to take care of, and now here we were with a family of our own.

It gave me such pleasure to watch Richard care for Emilio. He had always been a big-city, urban guy who dismissed the need to own a car. He grew accustomed to taking the train or bus to get around New York, San Francisco, and his hometown of San Diego.

Richard's job downtown was just a 15-minute bus ride from our home. Every evening around 6:00 p.m. Richard jumped off the bus at the last stop, a few blocks from our house. He ran those blocks as quickly as he could. One day, he was the last person to get off the bus, and the driver asked him, "Why do you run so fast the moment you get off the bus?"

Richard replied, "I am anxious to get home to my wife and my little boy. They are waiting for me!" The bus driver, obviously touched by Richard's words, said, "Stay on the bus. I am heading that way and will drop you off at your home." Richard told me later that he loved the idea because he knew Emilio would get a big kick out of watching his daddy jump off the bus right in front of his house! At two and a half years old, Emilio's favorite book was "The Wheels on the Bus." He also knew every word of that song.

The minute Richard walked into the house those fall and winter evenings of 1997, Emilio would shout out, "Hey dad, it's a good thing your home. Mom doesn't know how to make a perfect fire in the fireplace like you do!"

One of my favorite songs as a child was Julie Andrews' "My Favorite Things."

The following words raised my spirits whenever I felt sad: "I simply remember my favorite things, and then I don't feel so bad."

Waking up to Emilio every day was my most favorite thing to do. Nothing at all could make me sad now. Our time together transcended any of the highlights of my previous life. It was in my nature to be competitive at work. I still was that way; however, now I had something else, something more meaningful to think about. I found myself taking opportunities while driving or in between appointments to sit quietly and think about Emilio's progress and how far the three of us had come together as a family.

In the garden every morning, Emilio would say, "Mommy, look at this patch of grass. It's so pretty!" Where did he learn the phrase "patch of grass?" Only from a book or hearing his dad say this while in the garden together. He marveled over each flower that bloomed. Every sunrise or sunset we shared had a new meaning for me.

As Emilio grew and changed dramatically in his first three years, I was so proud of the little individual that he was becoming. I looked forward to every moment I had to be in his presence. His mind was inquisitive and filled with questions. "Mommy," he would say, "Why are the clouds so blue?"

"Well, Emilio," I would reply, "Because your daddy just finished painting the sky with your favorite color, blue."

He would laugh and laugh and finally say, "See, I told you that daddy had a stairway to heaven!" He loved these lyrics every time we played one of our favorite CDs, Led Zeppelin's 1971 "Stairway to Heaven." Among other attributes, he was indeed a very clever little boy.

As we moved along in our lives together, I knew that Emilio was teaching me many lessons. Lessons about how to love, be patient, and most importantly, live in the moment. That is how he lived. Every moment was noticed by Emilio. Isn't that what we all strive to experience?

Richard and I loved taking Emilio to the beach. He would gaze in wonderment at the expansive body of water flowing onto his little feet as we stood at the shoreline.

As each wave approached us, he was thrilled as Richard lifted him high into the sky to avoid the water from knocking him down. Emilio would laugh and squeal for more! "More waves Mommy, more beach!"

We loved spending Sunday afternoons at Uncle Gilbert's house on the beach. We gathered there with the rest of our Nares family. Emilio was the youngest grandson and nephew, and everyone loved spending time with this magical little boy. As he aged, his very blonde hair turned a soft honey-colored brown.

Emilio still loved to be held in my arms at two years old. Both Richard and I would carry him around everywhere we went. With our jogging stroller, we could get exercise on our weekend walks. Emilio would nap as we walked. It was always a wonderful time to catch up with one another and reflect on our blessings.

Even as a baby, Emilio rarely cried. He smiled all the time, and as long as one of us or Rosa came into his bedroom after his nap, he stood up in his crib with his arms out to be picked up, eyes smiling and full of love and affection.

There were moments when he had such an intense look in his eyes, a quiet knowingness as he observed his friends and his cousins playing around him. Sometimes he would smile, nod, and watch from a distance. It was not that he didn't want to engage, but his reactions seemed to be more about the fact that he got a kick out of watching the other children play, and then when he was ready, he would jump into the mix.

For Richard and I, observing Emilio was like watching a wise little man react to the world with humor and wisdom. We rarely shared these thoughts with others. We just found peace in his presence and knew in our hearts that he was a very special child. Emilio was our gift. He was divinely put into our lives at just the right time.

Richard worked on Saturdays and took Mondays off. Saturdays were very special for Emilio and me. They were a full day of spending endless hours together, just the two of us. We had a ritual of walking into the little village of our neighborhood and stopping for coffee and brioche at the French pastry shop. He was almost three and very talkative. He would politely order hot chocolate for himself, a cappuccino for me, and a warm brioche for us to share. I daydreamed about the future and how glorious it would be to duplicate this experience in a Parisian café in France, with Richard by our side.

Richard treasured his Mondays with Emilio. They always experienced new discoveries and shared them with me when I returned from work.

I occasionally traveled for my job. My overnights away from Emilio were tough, but I kept remembering that time was flying by, and I would soon be home enjoying his company. I found solace in that thought. I yearned to be home with my little boy with every flight and overnight hotel room.

Chapter 11
Remission Is a Good Word

Returning to that dreadful day when everything we knew to be true went sideways, we found ourselves searching for an ounce of energy that could push us in the direction of pulling ourselves together, if only for Emilio's wellbeing.

Memories of Emilio before his leukemia diagnosis flood my mind and take me back to those moments when we were safely together in our family unit of three. In a very short time, we found ourselves immersed in the truckload of books that were placed in front of us. It was our mutual quest to empower ourselves with knowledge about childhood leukemia.

At the end of the first 30 days of treatment, Emilio was in remission. Soon, a new set of words became our mantra. The doctor often repeated, "There are plenty of reasons to be hopeful, Mrs. Nares. Emilio's chemotherapy protocol is working."

Dr. Sudari explained that "Acute Lymphoblastic Leukemia is a blood disease. In childhood leukemia, the bone marrow produces abnormal white blood cells that crowd out healthy blood cells, preventing them from doing their job of fighting infection. Children with leukemia typically have one of three main types: acute lymphoblastic leukemia, acute myeloid leukemia, or chronic myelogenous leukemia. Emilio had the first type, ALL, the most common form of childhood cancer. The five-year survival rate in 1998 was 75%."

He encouraged us to be hopeful; as he spoke about these high statistics. Dr. Sudari told us about the global protocol treatment which would be used for Emilio because his leukemia was "standard, lower risk" rather than one of the other higher-risk leukemias.

I remember that an oncology nurse had been playing with Emilio in the playroom down the hall. She brought him back into the office to be with us at some point. Exhausted, he fell into my arms and closed his eyes. Dr. Sudari explained that Emilio would need to be admitted immediately and prepped for the surgery, which would insert a port-a-catheter into his chest. All chemotherapy, blood draws, and transfusions would be administered through his port-a-Cath for the next two and a half years of his life. This would eliminate the constant vein punctures, and needle pokes.

There is no possible way for a parent who is not trained in medicine to understand their child's cancer diagnosis. It is not the order of things. We should not be sleeping alongside our children in a hospital bed. It should be our hospital bed, our cancer treatment, not theirs.

Holding Emilio in my arms, I tried hard to keep him from seeing my tears. In a trembling voice, Richard said, "Come on, Emilio, let's walk down the hallway with Victoria and see our room." Pediatric Oncology Social Worker Victoria Grigg joined us at every step to ensure that we understood the medical jargon that had hit us fast and furiously.

Emilio cried, "I want to go home!"

"We will, sweetheart," I spoke as I choked on my words, "We just have to stay over tonight and get some medicine so that you can feel better." We reached his hospital room, and his eyes lit up as he saw the colorful and whimsical paintings on the wall. An oversized television set was hanging low for him to see. His nurse for that day had popped in a Barney video for Emilio to watch the moment he arrived in what would become his new bed for the following seven nights.

Next to his bed was a soft blue colored chair. It was an oversized, fairly comfortable chair that folded out into a bed. This would be the bed where Richard or myself would sleep during Emilio's overnight hospital stays. We were numb and unable to move forward. Within moments I had managed to change Emilio from his t-shirt and jeans into a child-sized hospital gown. Dr. Sudari arrived judiciously and gently explained to Emilio that he would comfortably fall asleep for a little while and that when he woke up his mom, dad, and Rosa would be with him, and that he could eat as much ice cream as he wanted to eat. I chimed in and told him that his favorite videos would be ready to play as soon as he came back to his room.

Emilio was in surgery for the following two hours. Victoria came back and directed us to the "Parent's Center." She explained that this area was a quiet place where we could wait until Emilio was out of surgery. Someone brought me coffee as I started the paperwork, and Richard raced home to pack our bags, one for me and one for Emilio.

Emilio's bag was filled with his favorite toys and stuffed animals. Richard assured me he would call one of our siblings and ask them to call the others and our parents. I would call my mother the next morning. I couldn't bear to speak these words; everything hurt so much. Little did we know that there would never be a right moment to share this information.

Richard returned moments before Emilio woke up in the surgery room. We found him screaming with a look of terror on his face. I felt so helpless and completely insecure about everything. I was angry because I couldn't help my son. My heart was broken, and my eyes were burning as my tears took up all the space in the hospital bed where time stood still as Emilio continued to scream. A nurse held his little hands together so that he couldn't pull on the tubes attached to his chest. He tried hard to get to his right thumb so he could put it in his mouth and find the comfort it had brought him every day and evening since his birth. "My baby, why you?" I begged God to take the cancer out of his body and put it in mine.

Emilio struggled with the constant flow of people entering his room. I.V.s needed attending to, a flow of medicines was given round the clock, and blood draws were taken every few hours. Richard and I moved into his hospital room. We slept by his side, praying he would be comfortable and get some rest.

It was difficult for our families to understand what Emilio was going through. They were so worried about him and wanted so much to be available to us. Someone was always present to pick us up when we fell, but how could they ever begin to understand what the future held for

Emilio. None of us knew the outcome. We couldn't even tell our parents and siblings what each new day would bring because we had no idea where that new day would take us. All we could do was put one foot in front of the other and walk into the current nightmare.

One particularly frightening day, I said to Richard, "I feel surrounded by the knowledge that we are living in the possibility of death, not life." It was so out of character for me to go to this place in my mind. Richard thoughtfully said, "The fear is overwhelming. Our minds will slip in and out of such thoughts. Promise me when I do this, you will help me switch the light back on, as I will do for you?" His wisdom astounded me.

At that moment, we held on tightly to one another and shifted the narrative that had started to take over that dismal afternoon. We began to concentrate on believing that a miracle would rescue us and save Emilio's life. We asked one sibling from each of our families to keep everyone else informed by email. Our sweet, aging parents did their best to understand what was happening to their precious little grandson.

My mom was always the first person I called. When I told her that Emilio had been diagnosed with leukemia, she cried with me on the phone until the two of us had no more tears to shed. My mom listened to me while I shared everything with her. Somehow, she knew exactly what I needed. Ever since Emilio was born, she was finally able to be the mother that I needed her to be.

I didn't want to hear anything other than her honest sorrow for me and my son. She had no answers and made no attempt to wrap it all up with a little pink bow. She had always been a realist; she had suffered great pain in her life, and I loved her so much for being exactly who she was with me.

My mom and dad visited us in the hospital several times during Emilio's first 30 days of treatment. When our favorite nurse, Lauren, walked into the room, she was startled to see how much I looked like my mom. She cheerfully said, "Mrs. Cappetta, it's lovely to meet you. For a moment, I thought that you were Diane!"

I have been told my whole life that I look just like my mother. Like most teenage girls, I never wanted to hear those words, but as I grew older, I began to view them as compliments. My mother, Mary was beautiful in a quiet, understated way, with dark, soft eyes and a Mediterranean complexion that served her well as the years progressed. Her jaw was angular, her cheekbones high, and her nose was narrow yet pronounced. She reminded me of the actress Sophia Loren. In fact, mom looked like Sophia Loren, although a bit more solidly built, and as she would say, "I have been cursed with the southern Italian stocky body frame of my ancestors!"

Our son quickly adapted to our new routine. He was relaxed and happy as long as we were all together. The hospital provided us with a psycho-social team that was tremendously supportive. They had a playroom for the children and a volunteer staff who helped get their minds off their illnesses. The skilled Child Life Specialists also played a large role in keeping life as "normal" as possible. Several parent liaisons visited us regularly. They are moms and dads who have experienced this situation firsthand.

They offered us great comfort, as did our nurses, who truly were exceptional. Not just anyone can do this work.

We were able to take Emilio home after nine days in the hospital to continue with medicines there. We nervously awaited the end of April when Emilio should be in remission. One of his primary medicines was the steroid Prednisone. It can rapidly kill leukemia cells. It tastes absolutely horrible, so after several attempts at feeding it to Emilio, we finally settled on mixing it with chocolate syrup and Sweet'N Low. Poor little guy. He would fight and fight and fight us like a pro wrestler until he knew he had to take it. This went on three times a day for 30 days. The consolation prize was that Emilio would be in remission once the Prednisone treatment finished. With hope in my heart, I gained some degree of strength to fight on.

I was so grateful for the understanding from my employer, and especially thoughtful throughout those first two weeks. The owners of the Importing Company that I was working for at the time of Emilio's diagnosis had a personal connection to pediatric cancer. They also had resources available for us and put me in touch with an organization. This foundation provides annual forums bringing in top doctors and scientists from around the world working exclusively on research for cures.

I woke up filled with fear the first weekend we were back home from the hospital. It surprised me how helpless I felt. It was Saturday, and Richard had to work. Saturday was always my special day with Emilio when I'd schedule play dates and visits to the Zoo or Children's Museum. This Saturday was different. I felt so afraid to expose our son to other kids. I sat quietly in bed with Richard's calming voice reassuring me Emilio's ANC total was HIGH. That was his "absolute neutrophil" count, which measures the body's ability to withstand infection. Generally, an ANC above 1,000 means a child can attend school and participate in normal activities. This blood count number is checked weekly to determine Emilio's activity level.

With a quick attitude adjustment, I gathered Emilio up, packed us a bag of goodies, and headed out to the park. I pushed him sky-high in the swing with abandon. As he giggled, I realized that my son was with me, he was having a good day, and I must enjoy these precious moments. The sun was shining on this beautiful Saturday in April, and my child, who had been through so much that month, was smiling. I reminded myself to hold tight to this memory and know we would get through this.

We blinked and hit the 30-day mark. Emilio was officially in remission! His ANC total was 1,500. He finished his Prednisone without losing even a bit of hair. We celebrated joyfully and thanked God for getting us this far.

About a week later, Emilio woke up with a fever. We were informed that if he hits the 101.5 mark, we must return to the hospital. This degree of fever signifies an infection that can only be treated with I.V. antibiotics. The hospital stays usually lasts three days.

I felt like I'd been pushed off a cliff. I'd returned to work now that we'd settled into our routine. I had appointments lined up all day. Although I was saddened that Emilio had a fever, I asked myself how I could possibly function as a working mother with such unpredictability in our lives. My beautiful son ran off to pack a bag with all his favorite toys, books, and movies. I was amazed by how gracefully he handled the situation. I gathered myself together and remembered I had Rosa's loving support. Once we settled in his room, I could head out to my appointments, checking in with Emilio and Rosa throughout the day.

There we were, in a flash, back in our home away from home, the hospital. Debi, our Child Life Specialist, and Rosa set up board games while Emilio's antibiotics were off to the races. Our nurse quietly assured me it was okay to stay focused on my life responsibilities. She reminded me these fevers do occasionally happen when children go through chemo. We were so fortunate to have Rosa and very supportive hospital staff. She was right. I must do what I need to do.

Emilio hugged me, smiled, and said, "Go to work, mommy. Tia is here with me." Where did this child get such strength of character? How does something so upsetting to me seem so alright with him?

Richard and I returned to the hospital around 6 p.m. that night. Rosa left, and we settled in with a home-cooked meal one of our friends dropped off. Emilio wanted us both to spend the night. We knew that sometime during the next two and half years, we'd have to start taking turns, but for now, we both stayed. The three of us played games, talked, and watched Disney movies until we all fell asleep.

Back home, after the fever subsided, life was somewhat normal. The chemo schedule kept rolling, and no other fevers occurred. Emilio's counts were fine, so he played with his friends, and spring turned to summer.

Even when Emilio went into remission four weeks after his diagnosis, and he stayed in remission for the following year and a half, I was still finding places to hide. I would sit in my car with the windows up and the stereo music blaring, or when I was working in my home office. When Emilio was at the park with Rosa, I would crawl into my bed and scream into my pillow, sobbing so hard that my eyes would swell, and my body would ache from the grief.

The combination of chemo drugs that put Emilio into remission was mild instead of intensive. So mild that Emilio did not even lose his hair. The chemotherapy that induced hair loss was not used in his two-and-a-half-year protocol. One would never know that he had leukemia just by looking at him. He was strong and athletic, keeping weight on. The only clue was the slight bulge in the middle of his chest where the port-a-Cath rested under his skin. It was hot outside, so his shirt was often off. Sometimes kids would ask about the bump.

"That's my port-a-cath. That's where the medicine goes," Emilio would say with a proud voice.

Kids accepted this answer and quickly moved on to something else like bugs or baseball. The loving response from neighbors, business associates, friends, and family were incredible. People continued to drop off hot meals, send cards, and just check in to see how we were.

One afternoon in the clinic, a little boy named David quietly sat up in the bed next to Emilio, waiting for his treatment to begin. He was four and a half years old, a year and a half older than Emilio. He and Emilio saw one another often in the clinic and loved playing Nintendo together. David was diagnosed with Neuroblastoma, a rare form of childhood cancer that starts in the nerve cells. The treatment for this type of cancer is very aggressive and lasts for ten months. David was very emotional on this particular morning, and tears flowed down his cheeks. He said to his mom sitting at the foot of his bed, "Mommy, why does Emilio have his hair and I am bald?"

Her response was sensitive as she explained, "That's because Emilio has a different kind of cancer with a different mix of medicines and different side effects."

I felt badly for David, but his mother's words reminded me that although Emilio still had his hair, which was a good thing for a child's emotional well-being, perhaps the mild treatment plan was not strong enough to keep his cancer cells away.

My advocacy about all issues that pertained to Emilio's treatment brought me right into the office of Dr. Sudari, who was on duty that day in the clinic. I explained my fears as he gently asked me to be seated. He said he had a few minutes and would be very happy to discuss the benefits of Emilio's protocol. He chose his words carefully as he said, "As you know Mrs. Nares, the global protocol treatment for ALL leukemia was established once a standard risk level was determined to be Emilio's status, the success rate is 75%, and this protocol is administered over a two-and-half-year time period."

He reminded me that I was always welcome to seek him out whenever I had questions. Of course, I knew that there were several social workers and psychologists available for parents to speak with about their fears and concerns. Still, it comforted me to hear these words directly from the mouth of a pediatric oncologist. Even though I knew I had taken a chance by storming into his office, he was in the middle of doing something else. I will never forget the power of this kind level of care that we received here at San Diego

Children's Hospital. It showed up many times as the future unfolded.

Putting my fears out of my head, for now, I tried to keep my mind from wandering back to my persistent habit of blaming myself.

In that first year, apart from blaming myself, I blamed God. I was so angry with him/her. How could I be so abandoned? As I finally had the chance to become a mother, how could my little boy, my miracle baby get cancer? I slipped into feeling sorry for myself, but only when I was alone. I continued never to show Emilio my fear, but he was intelligent and intuitive. He knew when I was afraid. "Don't be sad, Mommy," He would say, "I am having a good day!"

Emilio woke up every morning with a smile on his face. I woke up wanting to hold him and shelter him from what the new day would bring. His love held me up as we started to understand together what this "c" word meant.

In a very short time, Richard and I found ourselves resigning to the comforts of the new club that we had unwillingly joined. The comfort was found in getting to know other parents of children with cancer. Comfort also came from the nurses and hospital staff members who lovingly touched my hand, or smiled sincerely as they cared for my son, or without even asking me, would bring me a cup of hot coffee and a freshly baked cinnamon roll from the cafeteria. They knew that I was hungry even when I didn't care about eating.

If a parent found themselves caring for their child through cancer treatments, then you instantaneously became a valued member. In this club, in the oncology unit of our local children's hospital, I was surrounded by other parents who knew exactly how I felt. We became a tribe. We watched out for one another, cried together, brought coffee and snacks to one another, and even held each other's babies in our arms when one of us found ourselves collapsing with fear.

Chapter 12
Our New Tribe

One memory, in particular, guided my understanding of how empathy can go hand in hand with generosity.

It was a 10:00 p.m. chemo flush that Nurse Maria gave Emilio that particular evening. The two of us had just fallen asleep after his unexpected wake-up with a bout of nausea. When Maria finished, and Emilio fell back to sleep, I soon heard a soft voice at our slightly cracked hospital room door. "Diane, I am so sorry to wake you," she gently said. She, was ten-month-old Trevor's mom from the room next door.

I replied, "It's ok, Karen, let me come out in the hall, so we don't wake up Emilio." Tearfully, Karen told me that she had just received a call from her ex-husband Ben and he said he was picking up her two sons from her sister's house and taking them home with him.

Karen had been spending so much time at the hospital with their baby Trevor that she had been relying on her sister Kate to watch her other sons when Trevor needed an overnight hospital stay. Karen had full custody of her three sons. Her husband struggled to cope with the situation when Trevor was diagnosed with leukemia. He never showed up to assist her with clinic appointments or overnight chemotherapy treatments. That evening, she knew she had to leave and get her boys. Her husband had turned to alcohol and drugs in an attempt to cope with Trevor's illness.

Karen had obtained a restraining order against him. She did not believe that her other sons were safe in his home. The evening nurses told her to go and that they would watch over Trevor through the night. Two other moms joined us in the hallway while their children slept. The three of us assured Karen that we could take turns checking in on Trevor and help the nurses ensure that he was held and comforted if he woke up crying during the night.

This is what we did for one another. There was absolutely no more discussion. Karen left to deal with her challenging situation, and Trevor was comforted by three moms and two nurses whenever he woke up that night, as the IV poles hissed and the various chemo meds swirled around in the tubes by his bedside.

It was 3:00 a.m. when I heard him cry. I was relieved that Emilio was sleeping soundly as I crept out of his room and into Trevor's. I picked Trevor up and slowly danced with him around the tiny hospital crib. "Sleep little guy," I said. "Your mommy will be back soon." I didn't even hear Nurse Jennie step into the room. It reminded me how good a baby's skin felt against my chest. Tears flooded my eyes, and I once again felt the shock of knowing the incredible injustice of childhood cancer—a little baby suffering as he searched the room for his mother. My three-year-old son sleeps in the room next door, with an IV pole pumping chemotherapy into his body.

As Trevor's mother fights to keep her two little boys safe, I find myself screaming in a low, unrecognizable voice, "Where are you, God?"

This was our life, and only a parent who found themselves living within this horrifying world could ever be able to understand it. Reality check, this is real. You couldn't make up this story or the many other ones that took place in a pediatric oncology unit.

The following morning word on the floor was running rampant that three moms and the night nurses had spent the night before caring for the beautiful little ten-month-old baby, Trevor. The morning Parent Liaison on duty, Janelle Rodriquez, brought us a tray filled with freshly baked cinnamon buns and steaming hot coffee.

Janelle worked in the oncology unit, comforting parents because she knew intimately what they were going through. Janelle's daughter, Vanessa, was diagnosed with leukemia when she was two years old and was now a healthy, cancer-free teenager. Janelle not only brought us comfort food, but she brought us a reason to stay strong, a reason to be hopeful. Only through suffering can we ever find a way to appreciate the simple pleasures of life. As I showered and got ready to work, I was incredibly grateful for Janelle's gifts. The simple tray of love helped a group of weary moms forget their problems, even if it was for a few precious moments.

I was so happy to see Richard enter Emilio's room that morning. He had taken the day off to stay with Emilio until I returned from work. We were turning into a very efficient and loving team.

During Emilio's first year and a half in remission, we never, for a moment, thought that he would not beat his cancer. This was just a test, we told ourselves. We believed the three of us would come out of this experience with greater compassion and empathy for others' suffering. We just had to get through the two and a half years of treatment. When Emilio was cured, we knew that we would do something good in the world.

Meanwhile, we did what we knew we had to do. We strapped on our boots, headed out to the battlefield, and took our cues from our very special little boy. Where does a four-year-old child get the strength to keep a stiff upper lip while being poked and probed repeatedly?

Drifting in and out of our new normal, I couldn't stop thinking about Emilio's destiny. Having experienced this in his young life, God must be preparing him for greatness. No obstacle that life throws his way will ever get the better of him. He will be able to handle anything. Is that why he was chosen? Will all these children win The Nobel Prize, become President, or even cure cancer?

We played hooky from work on many of the good days and drove to the beach for long walks. When Emilio got tired, we would put him in his jogging stroller as he softly closed his eyes and took a nap. We often found ourselves checking into a hotel on the beach, close to home, to get away and feel like we were on vacation.

Emilio was so excited to swim in the hotel pool and get room service on our balcony which overlooked the beautiful, sparkling San Diego Ocean. There were many times that Emilio felt good while he was in remission. We always made sure that his friends came over to play with him as we celebrated all the good days.

In September, Emilio started preschool on a Tuesday and Thursday schedule, mornings only, to ease him into the transition. As long as his blood counts were good, school could help him live as normal a life as possible and develop socially. I knew that day would be emotionally difficult for him. I stayed with him, as several other mothers did with their kids.

The first week was pure hell for Emilio because he'd never been away from home, except for his hospital stays, but one of us was always with him. Preschool was a different story, with his leukemia in remission, on good days with high cell counts we wanted him to begin to have a sense of what it was like to be a four-year-old little boy. I insisted he stick it out, and if Richard ever got mad at me about something, it was that. I said Emilio needed socialization, and Richard didn't think that was a priority. Emilio would scream when we said goodbye. It was gut-wrenching for us. Richard and I would both cry when we needed to leave him.

It took several days before he would let Rosa, Richard, or I leave. After the second week, I settled him in, got up, and said, "Emilio, I too have to go to work. Just like you, I have to do my job. Rosa will be here to pick you up." I showed him the clock, so he would know when she would arrive. He cried and said, "Mommy, don't go!" It broke my heart, but I knew that he would be fine. School was an essential step for him.

Fortunately, Ms. Michelle, one of the teachers, saved his preschool experience. She said, "Come over here,

Emilio. I want to show you something." It was a table full of paint, glitter, and other art supplies. She also had a lifetime supply of golf balls the kids could paint and then roll. That was the only way he was able to stay. I called Michelle about an hour later. She said Emilio was upset for a few moments but then perked up as he got lost in imagination and creativity. From that day forward, as soon as he stepped foot into preschool, he made a beeline for the art room. If he made it into his creative sanctuary, Emilio could last until noon.

Emilio soon had his preschool buddies, and all was well. Subsequently, his days were jam-packed with sports and playdates with all his new friends. He had about two good months of ongoing preschool. He loved it. Unfortunately, school and the onslaught of winter brought on frequent colds. His blood counts remained consistently good, but it seemed like he caught a cold every other week. We couldn't risk developing infections, so attending school became an occasional treat.

Chapter 13
San Diego's Poster Boy

During the first year of Emilio's treatment plan, he became the "poster boy" for the San Diego Blood Bank. He was one of the children whose photos were displayed to remind people to donate blood and why their donation was so needed. Children with leukemia need blood transfusions regularly. The blood bank also focused on educating the community about the need for people to join the bone marrow registry. The only hope for an adult or child who relapses from leukemia and other blood-related diseases is to find a matching donor from the national and international registries. Several local children were featured in the blood bank's marrow drives to promote the need for a donor, just in case, these precious children were to relapse in the future.

Throughout Emilio's three-year journey with leukemia, various local news stations interviewed the three of us and heard our story. The news reporters and camera crew came to our house to do the interviews. Emilio would be shy for the first few moments, but then he would transform into a funny little character.

One day we received a call from my friend and customer, Lisa Busalacchi. Lisa invited us to join her for dinner with San Diego KGTV news reporter Jerry Medina.

We met on the patio of her restaurant in Little Italy. Lisa served us dinner while Jerry set up his cameras and microphone. Emilio was ravenous by 6:00 p.m. He was on the steroid prednisone that week, which left him starving most hours of every day.

As Emilio was eating his spaghetti, he decided to pull out his guitar and start playing songs for Jerry. Listening to Emilio sing, Lisa and Jerry began laughing hysterically. It was clear that Emilio wanted to get them laughing so that the cameraman wouldn't keep focusing on him. Within a few moments, they quickly remembered why they were doing the interview, and shifted gears into a more serious tone of voice. They wanted to know how Emilio was doing on his cancer journey. The interview aired a few hours later on the evening news. Emilio was still awake. He watched quietly then blurted out in his strong voice, "Mommy! How come Jerry only showed me playing my guitar for a quick second? He forgot to show me singing!"

When reporters came to our house, Emilio would take them into the backyard so they could film our garden, his playhouse, and watch him throw his baseball. They often called him a "funny little guy." Inevitably, viewers found him endearing, sending him get-well cards and letters.

Each year, hundreds of little fighters, warriors, and true champions at Rady Children's Hospital-San Diego battle one of the most formidable rivals of all: cancer. And each May, these champions are celebrated at one of the most inspirational events of the year: Celebration of Champions, a fundraising run/walk presented by the La Playa Unit of San Diego Children's Hospital Auxiliary.

Several of the San Diego Padres baseball team players were Emilio's sponsors over the years when we participated. They spoke to the media often about Emilio. They shared stories about how every time their own life took a challenging turn; they would think about Emilio Nares and quickly stop feeling sorry for themselves and be grateful for their children's good health.

Fatigued most of the time, Richard and I marveled that we were suddenly one year into this rollercoaster life that had consumed us. We counted the days on the kitchen calendar; one year of treatment left to go. We celebrated Emilio's fourth birthday on January 6, 1999. He'd been in remission for ten months by that point. Dr. Sudari told us we could have Emilio's Port-a-Catheter removed. He said many children continue the rest of their treatment program using a hand IV. Now that Emilio is a little older, this technique might be comfortable for him. We viewed this milestone as a signal that Emilio was closer to final treatment, although we were only halfway there.

Surgery to remove the port was difficult for Emilio. The anesthesia always made him sick. The soreness stayed with him for a few days.

Throughout my workday, most of my customers seemed in awe of our lives. I often needed to answer client calls while walking the hallways of the hospital with Emilio attached to his IV. I assured them Emilio would get through this. We would all get to the other side of this Everest. Richard and I carried on with faith and hope.

I continued working full-time while Emilio was in remission. I quickly learned that my state of being was a direct reflection, the mirror, of how Emilio was doing at any given moment on any given day. When his blood counts were low, Rosa kept him in the house watching movies and taking long naps. When his counts were good, she would put a mask on his face, and they would head to the park to play with his friends. This was Emilio's "normal" before it became a thing for the entire world to adapt to; 20 years later when in 2020, the COVIS-19 pandemic took over everyone's lives.

We spent our evenings together, cooking dinner, playing games, and settling in on the couch with his favorite videos. When Richard and I were not working, we only wanted to spend time with Emilio. Friends and family would call and offer to come and stay with Emilio. They all would say, "Go out you two, have some fun, relax and enjoy yourselves!" Honestly, an evening spent with Emilio uninterrupted was exactly what I needed to do at the end of a long, stressful day. He always brought me joy, and I always felt complete when I was with him. It was the same for Richard. We enjoyed life to the fullest on the good days and stayed very close to one another on the bad days. We hunkered down, nested in the warmth of our home. We dreamed about the healthy and joyful future that loomed before us. We were almost there.

An important business trip to Italy was on my calendar for June 15, 1999. I had become accustomed to taking one day at a time during Emilio's journey. Planning too far ahead was impossible; however, the trip was four weeks away, and I needed to commit to my company because the flights and hotel rooms were pending. Emilio's 15 months in remission was a milestone for all three of us. We were hopeful that Emilio would get through the next year of treatment in continued remission no matter how many "rollercoaster" rides he had to take to get there.

Chapter 14
A Familiar Journey

Richard and I made the decision that I would go to Italy. It was a ten-day visit to the regions of Tuscany and Piedmont. The agenda included a visit to several different wineries. Work trips such as this included time spent with families who owned some of the most prestigious wineries in Italy. I worked for a national company comprising sales and marketing people from around the U.S. My colleagues became close friends, and we traveled together yearly, relishing opportunities similar to this upcoming trip. The company I worked with from 1993–2002 was based in Chicago. Our team of 35 sales reps, managers, and VPs met at JFK Airport in New York for our connecting flight to Milan.

One of my favorite quotes is from Giuseppe Verdi: "You can have the universe if I may have Italy." I have always found Italy irresistible. From the first moment I traveled to this historic country at 19 years old, again at 23, and various times throughout my wine career, these inspiring experiences transformed me. Throughout history, Italians have turned their passion for living into an art.

No matter what region an Italian was born in, they speak with an obsessive pride about the glories of that place of origin. Twenty Italian regions make up the north, south, east, and west of this magical country which is the size of the state of California. The people of these individual regions proudly announce to each visitor that they have the finest cuisine and wine in the entire country!

My ten-day trip was splendid on many levels, although my mind wandered to thoughts of Emilio most of the time. In a postcard to Emilio, I wrote, "When treatment is finished, we will come to Tuscany together and take in all the beauty and peace it has to offer." Richard and I spoke by phone every few days, and he assured me Emilio was doing fine. Every time Richard called me, he spoke for a moment, or two, then was abruptly interrupted by Emilio. "Dad," he would impatiently say, "Let me talk to mom!"

"Mommy," he would quickly exclaim, "It's okay to have fun with your friends, but come home soon. I miss you!"

Each time I heard his words, I could not contain my tears. I would silently cry no matter where I was that day, standing in the middle of a vineyard tasting grapes or breaking bread while sitting at a long Tuscan table with my tribe of colleagues. I was fully aware that I was not making any sounds, but my eyes were filled with tears of fear just thinking about Emilio's cancer journey.

The trip started in Tuscany. Every morning at 8:00 a.m., we met on the terraced patio of our vineyard hotel. Each day began with a cappuccino, most often two, and slices of freshly baked bread just out of the oven. The bread was served with warm butter and various homemade jams. Waking up with the best coffee possible and the smell of the sweet breads, each one of us came to life as we reviewed the schedule for the day. Typically, one of the winemakers or a family member joined us for breakfast and took us on a tour of the vineyards. We strolled through each of the designated rows planted with various Sangiovese grapes. Three different soil types held the sleeping vines until it was time to pick the grapes at harvest in September.

The month of June was warm in the afternoon, but a cool sea breeze kept the grapes safe every morning and evening. Our daily lunches consisted of various courses that took us three hours to finish.

We always started with an antipasto of burrata cheese and various slices of prosciutto, salami, and crudo. A gorgeous Pinot Grigio was the perfect pairing for these assorted treats. A pasta dish soon followed, and every day the chef served a special sauce paired with a particular type of pasta. Our winery chef Luigi Solino loved to serve us seafood. Linguine with clams and shrimp was always my favorite. This exact pasta and sauce were Emilio's favorites too. I found myself smiling as I dished up memories of how much he loved to help me cook. "Mommy," he would say, "Please let me put the ladle in the pot of sauce. I love putting it on top of the spaghetti!" Then he would follow with the words, "I promise not to spill it."

One evening, Chef Solino made an outrageously delicious ravioli with wild boar. He shared with us that he only cooked with the wild boar that roamed the hillsides of this particular Tuscan property. The pasta was followed by roasted chicken or fresh white fish from the nearby Mediterranean Sea, and always a variety of sautéed vegetables garnished with the extra virgin olive oil from the estate. The baskets that held the crisp, salty bread were always replenished, along with a few bottles of the winemaker's latest creation. It was typically a Chianti Classico Riserva or a red blend of Sangiovese and Bordeaux varieties. Lunch finished with a slice of fresh peach or fig tart, an espresso, and a small serving of limoncello, and always a walk into the local village.

Indeed, everything was magnificent but always exhausting! Gratefully, each midday brought a small amount of time to return to our hotel room for a brief nap before the wine educational seminars, and blind tastings began. They lasted for three hours.

The challenging part of the trip was that despite the incredible meals and wine consumption, we still had to perform. The seminars involved questions and answers that always demanded our full attention. Many of the questions were asked of us individually and spontaneously. We did not have time to prepare savvy answers. We all got through it and ultimately joked with one another when we answered a question incorrectly. We were relieved when the time came for our 9:00 p.m. dinner, and we could relax again and enjoy ourselves.

Our Italian colleagues always professed that dinner would be "light."

"No worries," they would say, "Big meals are only served at midday; we always serve pizza and a salad in the evening." Although light, fresh, and healthy, these meals still consisted of more food and wine than most of us would consume in a single day!

My travel book for this trip was Elizabeth Gilbert's classic 2007 memoir "Eat, Pray, Love." Elizabeth wrote eloquently about her meals in Italy. She wrote about being miserable whenever her blue jeans were too tight, except when she was in Italy, it didn't matter. She described going out and buying a new pair of jeans, one size larger! Of course, she knew the next country on her agenda was India, where she would live in an Ashram and exist solely on a vegetarian diet. I lightened up on my obsession about trying not to eat so much pasta, "Really?" I asked myself. Instead, I went right into relaxed mode and enjoyed every delectable morsel.

I shared a hotel room with my good friend Cher Englestad. Cher lived in Orange County, just an hour and a half drive from San Diego. Our paths crossed often. She was a single mother of three daughters. Cher was well respected in the company and had always been a compassionate friend. I felt safe sharing my fears and anxiety about Emilio with her. She was with me the week Emilio was diagnosed and kept in touch with me throughout our journey. I was elated when the travel itinerary had us rooming together for the entire ten days. Cher knew my story: I could have never repeated the nightmares to a colleague from out of state, someone I didn't know very well. I just tried to stay calm and make it through each day until my flight took me home to Richard and Emilio.

The quiet moments of respite were minimal on this trip, but I tried to grab them when I could. Some mornings I would wake up before the rest of the group and take a short walk in the vineyards, absorbing the reality of my good fortune to be able to experience the loveliness that surrounded me at every turn. In these moments, I grounded myself and reflected on all the good pieces of my life. I had always been focused and driven to succeed in my work, and it was gratifying to be back in this world with my colleagues, if only for a little while.

On this trip, I had several powerful dreams about Emilio. In my dreams, his golden strands of hair kept getting in his eyes. Every time I would push them off his face, he would put his arms tightly around my neck as if he was holding on to me for fear of losing me. In my dream, I repeatedly told him, "I promise, Emilio, you will not break in my arms, hold on to me tighter. I will save you." I felt so responsible, and I just couldn't overcome the fear that I might lose him one day.

Our Piedmont visit was just as spectacular as Tuscany. The June weather was several degrees cooler, and the days were often covered in fog. This climate produced some of Italy's most powerful and unique wines. Geographically, Tuscany is located in central Italy, where the climate is warmer. Piedmont is northwest of Tuscany and borders France.

We started our visit with the elegantly regal wines of Tuscany and finished with some of the most highly rated, powerful Italian red wines from the villages of Barolo and Barbaresco. We studied and dined with two of Piedmont's most iconic winemakers, Angelo Gaja and Pio Boffa, of Pio Cesare Winery. My experience with these highly regarded Italian producers was one of the most memorable takeaways from my trip.

After the whirlwind days had finished, we caught an early morning train to Milan for our flight back to New York, where I would catch a connecting flight home to San Diego. By the time I could phone Richard from New York, he had taken Emilio on his routine weekly clinic appointment earlier that morning.

That appointment included Emilio's monthly bone marrow aspiration every other month to check his cellular activity. We had been through this particular test for well over a year, but nevertheless, we were always nervous at that particular appointment. I felt bad for Richard that he would have to go alone without me by his side, but neither my flight home nor this appointment could be changed. Emilio would be under full anesthesia for this procedure and wake up cranky and starving, but always with a clean scan.

While waiting for my flight home from a phone booth at JFK airport, I heard Richard's voice crack as he struggled to get the crippling words out of his mouth. Finally, managing to do so, he said, "Dr. Sudari is concerned about some suspicious cells that he found this morning in Emilio's bone marrow scan."

My only memory of the moments that followed our conversation was when I heard the boarding call for my flight, and as I stood up, my legs buckled under me. I struggled to control my breathing, and with my trembling words, I managed to tell Richard that I had to board my flight and I would see him and Emilio in six hours. As I hung up the phone, all I could feel was that paralyzing familiar fear that had become such an unwelcome part of my life. I sunk deep into my assigned seat, put on my eye mask, and cried all the way home from New York to San Diego.

Chapter 15
Entering a New Domain

Hearing the word "relapse" was far more devastating than accepting the initial diagnosis, "Emilio has leukemia." The three of us were called into Dr. Sudari's office the morning after I returned from Italy.

The doctor's face was a pale gray hue. Our favorite nurse, Beth, was trying unsuccessfully to hold back her tears. Susanna, the Child Life Specialist, came into the office and took Emilio gently by the hand. She said, "Emilio, I hear that there is a 'mean' pool game going on in the playroom. Come join me!"

He glanced back and forth at the two of us and quickly said, "Ok with you, Mom?"

I shook my head up and down and told him, "Absolutely, sweetheart, go have some fun, and we will see you shortly. We'll have lunch at McDonald's!" He was thrilled and skipped away with Susanna.

Dr. Sudari struggled to speak but finally got his words out. Almost whispering, and with his head down, he said, "Emilio's initial diagnosis of ALL leukemia came with statistics of 75% to 80% success rate for a cure. However, I am so sorry to tell you that, unfortunately, the global chemotherapy plan for Standard Risk ALL has not worked for Emilio."

As we had many times in the past, Richard and I found ourselves collapsing into one another's arms. But now, on this morning, one and a half years later, we knew too much. We prided ourselves in learning how to cope with Emilio's leukemia. His time in remission always reminded us that the success rates were high. After the terrifying shock of his initial diagnosis had begun to wear off and acceptance crawled in, our warrior spirits sprinted to the finish line. We had learned how to relish all the good days and safely retreat on all the tough ones.

We were devastated by this news and felt far more afraid now. I was heartbroken and experienced feelings of despair that were emotionally different than my initial emotions. Terrified, I cried out to Dr. Sudari, "What happens now? What is the next course of treatment when relapse happens?"

Dr. Sudari gently began to explain the next course of action. He said, "Emilio's relapse is the return of cancer cells in his bone marrow. There is only one thing that can be done. We need to find a marrow donor from the global bone marrow registry so that he can undergo a possible life-saving bone marrow transplant."

"One of us can be his donor, right?" I blurted this out since I knew absolutely nothing about bone marrow transplants. Richard and I worked hard to keep ourselves living in the present moment during Emilio's treatment. Call us naïve, but we honestly never thought that Emilio would not survive! We fought so hard to stay focused on our truths that hope always prevailed, and as long as the two of us believed in his survival, we would get through this bitter journey together, all the way to the finish line.

Dr. Sudari continued to explain, "Emilio's best chance at finding a perfect donor match is from a sibling. Since he does not have a sibling, the next step is to find a 6/6 chromosomal antigen match from the registry." I sank into my chair as my mind raced to thoughts of the two miscarriages I had experienced. In an emotional voice, I said to Richard, "Perhaps one of our other babies would have been a marrow donor match for Emilio?" I blamed myself again, and my old pattern of shame returned. Richard reacted to the news in a completely different way. He stood up and bravely told Dr. Sudari, "Let's get going. We have no time to waste. How do we begin this search?"

Although there were many additional information points Dr. Sudari needed to share with us, there was one point in particular that he seemed anxious to discuss. Gently, he started to speak, "Mr. and Mrs. Nares finding a perfectly matched unrelated donor from the registry is like finding a needle in a haystack. It isn't going to be easy. But we must remember that children and adults often find matching marrow donors and proceed to have successful transplants." Richard responded quickly, "What if we don't find a donor for Emilio?"

Answering this question was perhaps the one that scared Dr. Sudari the most. He said, "There is no avoiding the question of what happens next. While the search begins, Emilio will undergo a very intensive chemotherapy/steroid treatment plan. His side effects will be like nothing you have seen before, the pain will be more difficult for him to handle, but we have various medications to help manage it.

Emilio will need to come to the clinic twice a week rather than just one time each week. There will be more frequent hospital stays to treat his side effects and watch more closely for infections. This treatment plan will continue until we find a donor for Emilio."

Everything had changed. It was a different game now.

Containing our fear in front of Emilio was almost impossible. Richard and I had moments of despair, yet it seemed that when one of us went down, the other was up. This cycle continued, and we reminded one another that the only silver lining in this hideous situation was that we had one another and our like-minded philosophies about caring for Emilio. It was all about him; no one or anything else mattered.

Those in our orbit understood perfectly, and if anyone didn't, I had no interest in trying to explain it to them—my previous habit of putting on a good face no longer existed. We were living a life where nothing made sense. The only thing we could do was put one foot in front of the other and march on.

Chapter 16
The Donor Search Begins

The donor search originated from the University of California, Los Angeles (UCLA) labs. A specialized nurse, Lorraine Alvarez, led the team behind the search for Emilio's donor match. Two weeks into the search, she contacted me. She spoke carefully and with deep compassion. She said, "I am so sorry, Mrs. Nares, but we have not yet located a match for Emilio. I promise to contact you as soon as a potential match arises."

I was not sitting by waiting for her next call. I took it upon myself to call her every week. My initial words were the same, "Hello, Ms. Alvarez. You are checking the international registry, too, correct?" No matter how exhausted I was, I never seemed to be without a question. I continued to ask her, "How many new people join the registry each week?" Her reply was always gentle and affirmative. "Yes, Mrs. Nares, we are checking all the registries, and 1.4 million people are on the registry, with more joining every day. I promise to contact you as soon as possible." Thank God she was patient with me. I would collapse in despair if I had to defend my many calls with someone less compassionate.

While the search continued, Emilio began his aggressive treatment protocol. We were soon relieved and grateful that our insurance plan covered this treatment and the marrow search.

Emilio's hair started falling out immediately. My hairstylist, Lindsay, quickly rearranged her schedule to come to our house and give Emilio a buzz cut. The summer's trendy, cool buzz cut lasted eight days, and then he was bald. I kept putting his baseball cap on his head, yet he kept throwing it off as he screamed, "Mom, leave me alone! My head is too hot!" He couldn't care less about being bald at four and a half years old, but those feelings would change right around his fifth birthday.

Several pediatric oncologists have mentioned that if a child is diagnosed with cancer, the easiest time is infancy to five years old. Indeed, this was true for Emilio. We didn't get a sense from him that he felt different than other children until his fifth birthday. Then he became angry some of the time and took it out on his sweet little friends. He would yell at them while they were playing in the park. He was back on heavy doses of the steroid Prednisone, which made him agitated and anxious most of the time. He had little patience for the children whom he typically adored. Although most of them were surprised by his outbursts and would often cry, his best friend Blake always managed to stay patient with Emilio. I would hear Blake say to him, "It's ok, Emilio, you will get better soon, and then your hair will come back, and you will not be so sad." Out of the mouths of babes…

Emilio started averaging about three days of school each month when he felt really good. He loved to go, and watching him with the other children warmed my heart.

Emilio made it through the holidays without any drop in blood counts! We had a great Christmas with all his cousins and celebrated the year 2000, the millennium. It turns out the world didn't end!

I blinked, and my toddler turned into a five-year-old boy on January 6. We had a small party with four of his best friends whom he'd known since he was one. Rosa brought a piñata, and her daughter Rosita joined us too.

Emilio's greatest wish for his fifth birthday was to have a dog. We spoke with him about the importance of being responsible for his dog, treating them well, and helping us feed, walk, and play with the pup.

One Sunday afternoon, we met Sierra at a local animal shelter. She was a black and shiny, two-year-old Labrador mix. Emilio liked her because she was quiet while the other dogs barked incessantly, waiting for their new family to come and take them home. We brought Sierra outside to the shelter's fenced yard so Emilio could play with her. She scampered around him as he chased her and received his hugs beautifully. We liked her immediately and happily signed the paperwork.

Sierra's story was that she belonged to an elderly, sick man. No one in his family or neighborhood wanted to take her when he died. One of his nephews dropped her off at the shelter. She had been there a month when we found her. She seemed lonely and in great need of a companion.

Sierra was Emilio's dog, he became her master immediately, and I was her mama. Richard was a part of the pack, but not having grown up with a dog, he didn't know how powerful the human/dog connection could be. Richard loved observing the three of us at play, but I knew his plate was as full as he wanted it to be at that time. Richard never did anything halfway. He was always fully committed to the choices in life that he made. The two of us barely survived between getting to work each day and performing as best we could, managing our home, bills, Emilio's treatment schedule, and the numerous meds we had to juggle. Caring for a dog was a big deal, and between Emilio and myself, we had this one. Emilio wanted to be responsible for Sierra, and he excelled at caring for her on his good days.

Never knowing where the day would take us, we held on tightly to one another and rode the roller coaster ride once again, praying for something that could save our son's life. In that small window of time, that something was Sierra.

More milestones followed. Emilio was mastering his letters and numbers. The training wheels were soon to come off his bicycle, and Emilio learned how to ride a skateboard through the neighborhood.

Spending my days waiting for that call from UCLA was emotionally taking a toll on me. Not being able to concentrate on much else, I took a 30-day leave from work. On one of my more frantic phone calls, Mrs. Alvarez patiently said to me, "Mrs. Nares, Emilio's Latino background is one of the reasons that finding a match for him is so difficult. The registry is made up of less than 3% Latino Americans, African Americans, Asian Americans, and other non-Caucasian ethnicities." She continued explaining that it was essentially cultural and religious reasons, so many people did not join the registry. She compared it to giving blood or signing up for something that could be risky. "It is not for everyone," she said. She continued, "Some of Emilio's antigen chromosomes also reflect African-American markers."

We had searched the registry for one year, and a donor match had not yet been found. Heartbroken, we were beginning to come to terms with the fact that no one on the registry was a match for Emilio.

I returned to work, and we continued to care for Emilio through his intensive cancer treatments. I checked my messages daily for word from UCLA.

I was catching up on some paperwork in a Del Mar coffee house one summer afternoon. It was 3:30 p.m., and I found only one seat available upon arrival. This seat was at a long table that occupied a woman and a young girl. I asked the woman, "May I take this chair?" She kindly nodded and said, "Of course." As the little girl smiled, I realized that they were a mother and daughter reviewing homework at the end of the little girl's school day. She appeared to be about nine or ten years old. She had a sweet face with bright blue eyes that twinkled when she smiled. Her face soon turned somber as she exclaimed in a frustrated voice, "Mom, please help me with these questions. I am so confused!"

Trying hard to be discreet, I soon found myself unable to take my eyes off them. I had been having a pretty good and relaxing day until that moment. Suddenly, I could not find my breath. That familiar knot of fear was once again stuck in my throat. The darkness lodged in my heart, unable to move out from under it.

I began once again to ask myself the fearful questions, "What if I never share this kind of moment with Emilio? What if we never have the chance to talk about his homework? What if he never has the chance to go to kindergarten?" Complete and all-consuming sorrow engulfed me. Once again, I knew my little boy's destiny was clearly out of my control.

Within a short time, my ability to breathe returned, and I sat very still, sipping my water. Within a few moments, my legs regained motion. I slowly stood up, grabbed my notebook, and headed away from the mom's table and her seemingly healthy daughter. I was envious of their lives, and I didn't even know them. It would take me years to understand that almost everyone has suffered deeply. If they have not yet, they indeed will one day. The mom and her daughter stared at me, each with a kind glance, then they resumed their loving connection that I had been privileged to witness. Would I ever know a moment like that with my son?

Upon returning home that evening, I found Richard and Emilio lying on the couch watching the movie "Ironman." Emilio was giggling, and Richard kept tickling his tummy. Sierra was at Emilio's feet with her muzzle nestled against his toes. I waited a few moments, then dipped down to pick him up and held him in my arms. "Mom!" he shouted, "I'm watching my movie! Please put me back down on the couch!"

As I leaned back on the couch and closed my eyes, I reminded myself that Emilio was not gone. He was still here with me. There was still the chance that I would watch him walk to school, graduate from high school, head off to college, and get married. These were the same dreams that I am sure the mother in the coffee house had for her daughter.

After Emilio went to sleep, I shared my afternoon experience with Richard. He told me that after I left for work that morning, he was inspired to write me a letter. As he gently read it to me, I began crying uncontrollably. I soon covered my head in a blanket so I would not wake up Emilio.

Richard's words on paper were, "When I think of losing Emilio, I think of Diane more than myself because she is the MOTHER. Emilio and I had a close relationship, as contiguous as he and Diane, but there is something extra special about mother and child. The love I had for my mother, Emilio, has for Diane. I was the baby of the family and can relate so much because of what my mom meant to me. That's why Diane and I are together. That's why we're able to carry on because we are made for each other. We were strong going into Emilio's illness, and we're stronger coming out."

The intensive chemotherapy that Emilio endured in the first half of the year 2000 came with unbearable side effects. Most days, Emilio was in discomfort. At one of his clinic visits, Dr. Sudari said, "There is a bi-monthly treatment that Emilio will need. Emilio will not have to come to an outpatient visit just for this treatment if one of you could administer this medicine yourself?" I didn't even need to think about it. I looked Dr. Sudari right in the eye and said, "Yes, of course, anything that we can do at home to avoid bringing him to the clinic is fine with us. What do we need to do?" Proud of being so direct with him, I soon found myself shaking uncontrollably with a petrified look on my face.

Dr. Sudari explained that this particular chemotherapy, Peg Asparaginase, was administered through a shot in Emilio's right thigh. He continued, "A transformative product called Emla is available and will numb the place on one's body where the shot needed to be inserted. Emilio will feel a slight pinch when the shot goes into his leg, but the kids tell us that they feel nothing else after that."

Wow, I couldn't wrap my head around what it would be like to stick a massive needle in my little boy's leg. I knew the experience of doing this would be traumatic for all three of us. I nodded my head Richard's way and assured him that I would be the one to give Emilio his leg shot. Although Richard is always heroic, he seemed relieved to hear my words.

Dr. Sudari said, "I am very pleased to hear this. It will mean a lot to Emilio to have one less day to come to the clinic." I, too, was relieved and prayed that my home care for Emilio would soon become routine and not such a devastating experience. Dr. Sudari arranged for a home-care nurse to arrive at our house the following morning at 8:00 a.m.

Nurse Kathy showed up on time and brought a vial of this potentially life-saving medicine. Her bag also included the needle, bandages, tape, and most importantly, the Emla numbing cream. Kathy patiently taught me how to administer this leg shot to Emilio. The plan was for her to return one additional time, and then I would be on my own every other week for a three-month cycle.

Somehow, I found the strength to give my son what he needed at this time. I couldn't think about what I had to do. It just got done.

The first time I gave Emilio this shot, Richard held him down as he cried and screamed. "No, Mommy, no!" It broke our hearts, and we cried along with him. By the third time, we had turned the shot into a game. Together, the three of us took a long, deep breath and held it for 10 seconds as I administered the shot. Richard ran to the kitchen to pull an ice cream cone out of the freezer. Emilio smiled and ate his ice cream; suddenly, all was right with the world.

One afternoon our next-door neighbor, Leo Devine, knocked on the door. Leo and his wife, Katherine, constantly checked in on Emilio. They moved into the neighborhood two years after we did. The two of them met one another several years after losing their spouses. Leo's wife was lost to cancer, and Katherine's husband to divorce. Leo came to the marriage with two high school children and Katherine with two sets of twin boys. We loved watching this large, active family play in the alley behind our homes. Leo and the boys joined Richard and Emilio often as the eight of them practiced pitching and hitting baseballs. Katherine was a compassionate woman who took her golden Labrador therapy dog, Molly, to Rady Children's Hospital oncology unit to visit. Emilio was always excited to see Molly at the hospital.

Leo visited us that afternoon to share news about his recent search to help us find a donor for Emilio. Leo had been spending a great deal of time reaching out to his medical colleagues around the country. One of his colleagues told him about a pediatric oncology team doing a unique transplant for children like Emilio who could not find a bone marrow donor. Leo did his homework, and through his research, he discovered some intriguing information. The lead oncologist and her team were at Boston Children's Hospital. They were the only pediatric oncologist/researchers doing a Phase 2 Study in the country. This special transplant is a half-matched stem cell transplant from a family member. The donors can be the patient's parents, children, siblings, and sometimes cousins. A biological parent or a biological child is always a half-match to the patient based on genetics.

The results of this transplant showed a 50/50 success rate with 22 children. Emilio would be the team's 23rd patient. The transplant had been in effect for only two years, as it needed time to receive Phase 2 status. This short time made it challenging to gauge long-term success.

We told Leo how we would go anywhere in the world to save Emilio's life. We nodded in agreement that we would never be able to forgive ourselves if we did not get on the quickest flight to Boston and meet with the team to see if this would be a good option for Emilio. Leo was not the least bit surprised by our words.

Three days later, we found ourselves on a flight to Boston. Neither one of us had ever been there. We shared a strong desire to visit this city together one day. We never thought that our first visit would be to meet with a renowned pediatric oncologist to discuss a bone marrow transplant for our only child.

We cleared our work calendars for the following two days and arranged for Rosa to stay with Emilio. We made an appointment with the transplant assistant and had all of Emilio's paperwork faxed immediately to her office.

Bleary-eyed, we landed in Boston on a red-eye flight from San Diego. It was already a warm, humid early August morning, the summer of 2000. We sat in the lobby of the hospital near downtown Boston.

A strikingly lovely woman with kind eyes approached us. Along with a cup of coffee, she held Emilio's medical records in her hands. Although it was hot outside, the clinic and hospital unit were chilly from the constant running of the air-conditioning. Dr. Guinan protected herself from the chill of the clinic by wearing a short, chocolate brown leather jacket and a flowing "bohemian-style" long floral skirt. She was stylish with her lovely dark hair and her petite, fit shape.

When she smiled, her face lit up with warmth and compassion. Her eyes twinkled as she looked deeply into our eyes, revealing this transplant's positives and negatives that she so deeply believed in as an option when there was no other. Her warmth continued filling the space surrounding the three of us as we sipped our coffee and listened to her speak about this groundbreaking transplant.

There was nothing else. We had to try it.

Richard felt exactly the same way. Everything about Emilio's journey with cancer was devastating beyond what words could express. Still, one thing that kept coming back to us was that we would have remorse and deep regret if we did not try an available option that had a 50% chance of working.

Dr. Guinan's assistant Liana joined us and provided a book about the transplant and Boston Children's Hospital. We met the team of oncologists and nurses who would care for Emilio. We toured the hospital grounds, spent time in the healing gardens, and prayed in the chapel.

We weren't blind to the fact that this transplant had its challenges. One of us as a donor was not the "perfect" match for Emilio, but the apheresis collection of Emilio's healthy cells being put back into his body offered hope. We kept returning to the fact that this team had a 50/50 success rate. The only statistics we had been hearing the entire year were from pediatric oncologists who continued to tell us, "I am so sorry, Mr. and Mrs. Nares, without a transplant, Emilio may have a 15% chance of surviving another year." At this time, even a ray of hope offered a sense of relief.

After our appointment, we took Dr. Guinan's advice and visited the Isabella Gardner Museum, followed by dinner in an Italian restaurant on Newbury Street. Both experiences were invigorating. We found ourselves breathing normally for the first time in a very long time. While sipping a delicious Italian red wine, Richard leaned over and said, "Is it ok to feel a sense of relief? Might Emilio really have a chance at life?" I nodded and responded with a deep exhalation, "I think so."

I had almost given up on being able to say these three little words of hope.

We flew home early the following morning.

Chapter 17
The Possibility of Hope

Six hours later, we walked into our house, held Emilio in our arms, and told him the story of a new hospital and a new doctor who would help him get well. His first words were, "Can I bring Sierra?" My heart skipped a beat, and all I could say was, "Sweetheart, we need Sierra to stay home and take care of our house. She will be here waiting for you when we return." He seemed okay hearing my words and quickly changed the conversation to a discussion of flying on an airplane all the way to Boston! With a firm voice, he said, "Mommy, I want to bring my CD player so I can listen to my music with the airplane headset, and remember, I get to sit by the window!" His bossiness never sounded better than it did at that moment. All I could say was, "The window seat is yours, my precious son!"

Within the following three weeks, we arranged a leave of absence. Dr. Guinan told us that it would be impossible to know exactly when we would return home. Recovery from a bone marrow transplant could take about three months, but it was sometimes longer. Both of our employers assured us that we would have our jobs back whenever we returned.

My employer gave me eight weeks of partial leave salary, which would help tremendously. I was so grateful, but with each passing day, I became incapable of being able to concentrate on anything but Emilio. I found it impossible to comprehend that I could get up every morning, put my work face on and go out into the world and sell wine. Fine wine is a luxury brand, one of life's sweet pleasures, but it seemed so insignificant in my world at that time.

I was grateful for all the love and support I received from my company, my customers, and my colleagues during this continual nightmare that would not let me rest. My baby was an extension of myself, and the thought of him suffering knocked me off my feet. I barely survived those days of uncertainty, and at the end of each one of them, I prayed that I could get out of bed the next morning for Emilio's sake. He needed me. It was pure and simple. It was inconceivable that I could ever let him down.

Dr. Sudari often spoke with Dr. Guinan as he prepared Emilio for his transplant. It was imperative that Emilio stay in remission for him to undergo the transplant. Emilio had been back in remission for the past two months. Some additional rounds of intensive chemotherapy would ensure that the remission remained in place for Emilio to transition to Boston.

Richard and my health records were sent to Dr. Guinan so that she could determine which one of us would be the best donor match for Emilio. We both wanted to be Emilio's donor. It would have been an honor for me to do this for my son, but Dr. Guinan gingerly informed us that typically when a dad is a healthy person, as Richard is, he would be viewed as the preferred choice. She explained what I already suspected, that women's internal systems due to pregnancies and miscarriages can complicate the situation. I had no trouble understanding this logic.

Richard was filled with pride that he would be able to donate his marrow and become Emilio's donor. He viewed this as his greatest gift to his son.

Our community of friends rallied to assist us in many ways. Our sister-in-law, Sally, had a niece who had recently moved to San Diego. Claire was free to be able to stay in our home while we were gone. Claire was a huge dog lover, so she was thrilled that Sierra was a part of the package.

Emilio knew he was going to a new hospital with a new doctor who would help him get well. He was sad to leave his Tia Rosa. Rosa told him she would come to see him in his new hospital. He was so excited and talked about her every day. Emilio was also sad to leave Sierra. We brought lots of photos of her, and he drew and painted pictures of her every chance he got.

Chapter 18
A Second Chance

The three of us flew to Boston on August 26, 2000.

There was no turning back. Turning back meant we would be taking our son home to die. That was not an option for me, and gratefully Richard felt the same way.

We packed two suitcases for ourselves, but we needed to purchase one giant suitcase for Emilio. When Emilio saw how big his suitcase was, he quickly said, "I am going to call this the big black suitcase!" Our two bags held the contents of what we would need to live in Boston for three months or longer. We would finish the summer season and have the privilege of witnessing the New England leaves on the trees turn to exquisite colors of rust, gold, and orange. These were colors that we rarely saw in Southern California.

Richard and I didn't need much beyond what we referred to as our "hospital wardrobe," which consisted of comfy, oversized sweats and sweaters for the chilly hospital room and a few tanks, shorts, and sandals to endure the remaining Boston summer heat and humidity. But Emilio's big, black suitcase held a few articles of clothing but mainly his favorite toys, videos, and stuffed animals. We wanted him to have all of his favorite things, hoping that this could bring him some comfort.

On that warm summer morning in August, two neighbors, Diane and Veronica, picked us up and drove us to the San Diego airport. They also took care of making reservations for us at the Boston Ronald McDonald House, where Richard and I would take turns living while Emilio was in the hospital.

Friends donated their mileage points for our flight. Emilio sat next to me, and Richard was across the aisle. Emilio loved sitting next to the window so that he could watch the enormous wings of the plane. Throughout most of the six-hour flight, Emilio listened to his favorite musical tapes with his headset. He had never really understood the concept of whispering, so he happily sang out loud without realizing that people nearby could hear him. His voice was so sweet, and he was always smiling.

No one at all seemed to mind.

It was pretty obvious to most of the people on the flight that the little boy in the front row, next to the window, had cancer. As usual, I kept putting his baseball cap on his head, and he kept taking it off. It made his head hot, and it was a very long flight.

I was more bothered by Emilio's bald head than he ever was. I didn't want other children or adults to stare at him. I never wanted him to feel different. He was not too uncomfortable in the face of adversity, but I certainly was. I was his mother, and I couldn't bear it if he had his heart broken by the stares or unkind words of strangers.

A hot lunch and a glass of chardonnay were a welcomed distraction for Richard and me. I settled into the reality that there was hope in Boston. Stepping into the unknown was always fearful, but what choice did we have? We either had to jump in with energy and positive thoughts or curl up and die. Given that we both had chosen to jump in wholeheartedly by taking Emilio to Boston for a special transplant, we dismissed our fear and took a leap of faith.

Upon our arrival in Boston that first evening, we headed to a hotel room at the Best Western, located across the street from Boston Children's Hospital. Veronica had also booked this for us, knowing that our flight to Boston would arrive late in the evening and Emilio's first clinic appointment was 7:00 a.m. the following morning.

Emilio was exhausted and cranky when we had to wake him up to get to the clinic on time. He was unhappy and rude to Dr. Guinan's assistant, Liana, as she tried to comfort him. He looked sternly at her and said, "Don't touch me. Leave me alone!"

We were mortified!

Emilio's reaction was completely out of character. We apologized to her and reprimanded him by saying, "Emilio, you are being very rude to someone who is just trying to help you. Apologize to Liana right now!" With his head bent low and seemingly nervous, he said, "I am sorry, Liana, I am just very tired." She wrapped her arms around his little body and replied, "It's okay, Emilio, of course, you must be so tired, having flown on a big airplane across the country!"

She continued to tell him that he deserved a big "hall pass" and that she knew he was a great little boy. I knew that he had no idea what a hall pass was, but being a typically well-mannered child, he shook his head up and down as if he was grateful for the kind tone in her voice. He managed to give her a warm smile.

Within a few moments, Dr. Guinan joined us. I could tell that Richard was feeling as shaken up as I was. We rarely had to reprimand Emilio. Witnessing his exhausted face and our sleep-deprived expressions, the doctor made Emilio's first appointment very brief. She said, "There is really nothing that needs to be done right now. Emilio, just a quick check-up and a blood transfusion will pump you up with red blood cells and give you plenty of energy to get through the next three days of fun in Boston!" Emilio appeared to like his new doctor immediately. Although he had no idea how to pronounce her last name, he moved his little face close to hers and said, "What should I call you?" Dr. Guinan gently said, "You can call me Dr. Lilly. That is my first name."

He seemed to be incredibly relieved. His temper had softened as he threw a quick glance and another smile at Liana. She told me later that she was very used to the children's mood swings. She said, "Mrs. Nares, with all the medicines and steroids our children have to live with every day, it's no wonder they display frustration and anger, poor darlings." We were definitely being cared for in Boston, as we were at home in San Diego. With a deep breath and sigh of relief, we settled into our new life.

Emilio's energy level rose several notches when he heard the surprising news from Dr. Guinan that the next three days and evenings were free for us! She told us to enjoy the city's sights, play, and rest. She informed us that we would see her again at the hospital check-in on

September 1. She gave us her cell number and insisted that we call her if we had any concerns.

During those three "free" days, we moved into our new home, the Boston Ronald McDonald House.

Families worldwide traveled to Boston Children's Hospital to have their children treated for cancer. We were fortunate that the Ronald McDonald House was available for families to live during these incredibly challenging days and nights. The Ronald McDonald House program allows parents far from home to stay close to their children who are spending endless days in the hospital or going to outpatient clinic treatments daily.

"The House" as it was lovingly referred to, was a big, three-story, 1920s Victorian located one mile from the hospital. It had been renovated but still possessed the cozy charm of an old Brookline, Massachusetts estate. The oversized front porch was a welcoming place to land at the end of each day. The walk from the hospital to The House was lovely, but a shuttle was always provided to transport families back and forth in the evening or when they were utterly exhausted, which was most of the time.

Emilio slept at The House with us for the following three evenings. On our fourth day in Boston, he was admitted to the hospital for his transplant prep. He got a big kick out of the basement of the house, which held an ice cream parlor that opened up every evening after dinner. It was a perfect end-of-the-day, relaxing place to be for the children and their families on those hot, humid August nights. Emilio was elated when we left the basement and took our ice cream cones to the front porch with the large, charming, oversized swing.

I sat quietly watching Richard hold Emilio in his lap as they held on tightly, swinging back and forth. That evening, on the expansive front porch of The House, the three of us experienced a few moments of relaxation. It was a time to not worry about what the upcoming days would bring. Exhausted but content, I imagined we were just a mom, a dad, and a sweet little boy from California on vacation in Boston.

The backyard of The House was filled with toys, swings, and slides that nestled up against the woods on a one-acre property line. A local women's group brought home-cooked warm, fresh dinners to The House most evenings.

Each family was provided with its own section in the spacious kitchen. Standing in my designated space, in this giant kitchen, was one of the few times I would experience a sense of control over my life. We shopped for our groceries in the open-air market nearby, and I found comfort and solace when I cooked a hot meal for my family.

Boston Children's Hospital was at the forefront of cancer care. As one of the most well-respected cancer centers in the world, it drew people from around the globe.

The House filled up quickly, and we were fortunate to have a room there for as long as we needed. I loved the smell of the exotic aromas coming from that kitchen at the end of every challenging day. Moms and dads could be found prepping and cooking meals from their homeland. During our time in The House, we met families from China, Japan, Eastern Europe, various southern European countries, and from all over the United States.

Our spacious room had three twin beds and included our own bath and shower. The room was ours at a mere cost of $5.00 per day. I have no memory of ever paying for this. It was obvious that my girlfriends took care of this cost for a while. Knowing their kindness, I suspect that the remainder of our stay was covered by loving neighbors, the same ones who cooked for us when Emilio was first diagnosed with leukemia.

In the spring of 1998, our friend Diane arranged a neighborhood cooking schedule. Every evening for the first two months after Emilio's diagnosis, a hot meal arrived at our front doorstep. If we were sleeping that evening at the hospital, then Diane would inform the particular cook for that day to help find a way to get it delivered to the receptionist's desk at Rady Children's Hospital-San Diego. These meals meant the world to us. These gestures of love and support were abundant and continued in one way or another throughout Emilio's cancer journey.

In the kitchen at The House, we were each given brown grocery bags and a marking pen to write our names in big letters on each bag. We kept our groceries and snacks in the refrigerator and cupboards. Everyone respected one another's space.

None of us had woken up from the nightmare we found ourselves living in. We just went about caring for our children, as they lived in a compromised situation day after day, year after year. None of us was immune from the pain. We just didn't have the strength to put it on display. We were far from home, uncertain of how long we would be there, and unsure of the outcome.

As difficult as it was to do, most of the moms and dads remained positive and hopeful when we were in that kitchen. When one of us was falling apart, and inevitably every one of us did, several times, a skilled counselor or nurse would whisk us away to a safe and isolated place in the garden. The garden became a safe place where we could cry, scream, or simply collapse from fear. These compassionate professionals held on to us tightly until we could breathe again. Apart from having a massive support system, we also had one another.

On the tenth evening, since Emilio's transplant began, it was my turn to return to the house to sleep. It had been a particularly grueling day for Emilio as bed sores, and severe swelling began to settle into his body. Emilio had been suffering from new symptoms for the past ten hours. Richard's bone marrow had started the process of engraving into Emilio's body, and Emilio's cells were rejecting the host cells, which would take place over a period of time until the engraftment was complete. The whole process was overwhelming and frightening, yet ultimately life-saving.

Richard's arrival would relieve me for the night, but any sleep looked grim for him and Emilio. Our well-organized schedule would fall apart once again. It seemed like an eternity until 5:00 p.m. when Richard arrived back at the hospital.

As we caught up with one another about Emilio's status that day, I remembered that the last shuttle back to the house would leave the hospital shortly. Typically, the parent sleeping at The House would stay at the hospital and get dinner from Au Bon Pain Café on the bottom floor. The food was delicious, and dining together, if only for 30 minutes, was the only bright light at the end of the day. But that evening, I wasn't interested in dinner.

I waited until Richard could run downstairs to bring up some food, and I was anxious to get back to the House to eat my home-cooked leftovers. I had to get out of that room, but I didn't feel capable of walking back to the House. As soon as Richard returned, I grabbed my coat, kissed him and Emilio goodbye, and told him I needed to catch the shuttle. I jogged out of the unit and flew downstairs to the main entrance. Our evening nurse called the lobby attendant to ensure the driver had waited for me.

Gratefully he had, and I thanked him as I dashed into the open side door of the shuttle. The driver quickly headed out of the valet space and onto the highway toward the city. Although I was heading to the back of the bus, I quickly turned around and walked back to the front. Feeling beat up and downtrodden, I composed myself and said, "Excuse me, sir, I know that I was late, but I am staying at the Ronald McDonald House just one mile away in Brookline. Can you drop me off before you head into Boston?" His tone was gentle as he replied, "Of course I can; just take a seat and rest."

He must have understood my unstable condition. This was his job, and apart from taking hospital employees to the bus or the train station, he shuttled weary, frightened parents to and from the hospital every morning and evening. He turned the bus around and headed back into Brookline.

Suddenly I heard a woman's voice from the back of the bus shout, "Hey where are you going? I have had a long day working at the hospital and need to get to the train station!" Before she could get any further words out of her mouth, the woman seated next to me rested her hand on my shoulder, stood up, and said, "This woman has just left her sick child in the bone marrow transplant unit after a harrowing day filled with fear and worry. The driver is dropping her off first and then he will head into Boston."

The silence was deafening. Timidly, the frustrated woman told me how very sorry she was. Sitting back in her seat, she said, "I apologize. I just wasn't thinking. Please forgive me." As it turned out, the woman who spoke on my behalf was a nurse in the same unit where Emilio was being treated. We had not met her yet, but she clearly knew who we were.

I was back at the House in just a few minutes, climbing the stairs to our room. I was so exhausted that I did not realize at that time how devastating the shuttle experience had been for me. I knew that it would be wise first to grab some food and warm it up for me to be able to sleep that night. I walked back downstairs and into the kitchen. It was a Wednesday evening, and I had forgotten that the local women's church group would be in the kitchen cooking dinner for the families.

I didn't want to talk to anyone. I avoided eye contact until one of the women approached me and asked if she could make me a plate. Before I had the chance to run out of that space and isolate myself, I could feel the blood rushing out of my face, and once again, my legs collapsed beneath me. One of the moms nearby lifted me and settled me into a comfortable chair in the den. She simply knew by looking at me that I was feeling the same paralyzing fear she had on numerous occasions during her 10-year-old daughter's cancer treatments.

It's as if every cell in your being is being ripped apart. Nothing stays together because you're just completely destroyed. Tears flooded my eyes and streamed down my face and although I was famished, I couldn't eat a morsel. She packed some snacks for me from her cupboard and guided me up the stairs to my room.

I cried myself to sleep and couldn't even imagine how I could speak my words of fear the following morning back in Unit 6 with Richard and Emilio. I felt frozen in time and eventually drifted off to sleep until I awoke the next morning at 7:00 a.m. when the alarm went off. All I could think about was walking back to Emilio and watching him endure another day of pain and discomfort. I felt completely helpless.

Chapter 19
Freedom in Boston

During our free days in Boston before Emilio's transplant began, the three of us enjoyed visiting the many historical sites of this mesmerizing city. Although Emilio was often tired, he amazed us with his ability to keep on going. He was determined to get the most out of each one of these days. We cherished this private time with him, always knowing how precious it was and that each bright moment could turn dark at any time. We took nothing for granted, as we found our spirits renewed in his presence. We never wanted the day to end.

We began our first day shopping in Beacon Hill's famous grocery store and deli, Dean & Deluca. We bought goodies for a picnic in Boston Commons Park. While waiting in line, Emilio said, "Mommy, I am so happy that we chose the Brie cheese instead of the Italian cheese. The Parmigiana has a very strong smell, and I want to smell good today because I am so happy."

Several young pre-med students wearing scrubs were behind us in the grocery line. They appeared to be from Harvard (one of them was wearing a Harvard sweatshirt). This was Boston, the mecca of medicine at its best.

The students smiled at Emilio, getting a kick out of this cute little boy with cancer. It was hard to miss his little bald head underneath his Padre's baseball cap. His gentle face was swollen, as it always was, after steroid treatments. The dreadful steroid Prednisone was still part of his monthly protocol.

A friend of my brother John gave us tickets to see the Boston Red Sox take on the Detroit Tigers. Richard and Emilio were elated because baseball was their favorite sport.

During the seventh-inning stretch, the marque announced a warm welcome to Emilio Nares from San Diego, California! Chills ran down our spines as we pointed this out to Emilio. He smiled shyly. As he buried his head into Richard's shoulder, he said, "Daddy, how do they know I am here?"

"It must be a gift, Emilio, from your Uncle John," I explained. Little did we know then how much Uncle John's gift of himself would serve us.

On our last "free" afternoon, we saw the Van Gogh exhibit at the Boston Museum of Art. Richard was a huge Van Gogh fan. When he painted, he always wore his Van Gogh "Self Portrait" T-shirt. As we stood in front of this great work of art, Emilio pointed at the painting and whispered, "Look, Mommy, it's Daddy!" A few feet away, he moved toward Van Gogh's Sunflower painting. This time Emilio shouted loudly, "Look, Mommy, it's Daddy again!"

Richard was a master at painting sunflowers. Emilio got to see his dad's work in the homes of several of our family members and friends.

That evening, I held Emilio in my arms and couldn't let go. Deep in my fear, I could no longer calm myself. I would soon lead him into Dante's Inferno, a place of darkness before the light, hope, and dreams could return.

There was no preparation for what was soon to take place. We dove in head-first and prayed that we would not hit bottom before we were resurrected.

Chapter 20
A New Birthday Begins

We were told a successful bone marrow transplant gave the patient a new birthday, a new beginning. Emilio's new birthday would be September 3, 2000, the day his father, his donor, would rescue our son, giving him new and healthy cells.

We woke up early on that warm, humid first day of prepping Emilio for his upcoming transplant. We packed two bags, one for Emilio that included some of his favorite toys and videos, one outfit for him to wear to the hospital, and another one to wear back to the Ronald McDonald House when his transplant was finished.

The other bag was for me. I was the one who would stay over with Emilio on his first night. Richard and I proceeded to alternate nights, sleeping beside Emilio's bed on a fold-out sofa chair.

A shuttle picked us up, and Dr. Guinan met us on 6 West, the bone marrow transplant unit. While Emilio played with one of the Child Life Specialists, Dr. Guinan explained the course of activity for the day.

The first order of business was to spend several hours in the Apheresis room with two specialized technicians. We could both be in the room with him the whole time. A nurse prepared two chairs for us.

Apheresis is the removal of blood plasma from the body by the withdrawal of blood, its separation into plasma and cells, and reintroduction of the cells, used specially to remove antibodies in treating cancer and autoimmune diseases.

For Emilio, his healthy cells would be injected back into his body to help kill off his cancer cells. Emilio's blood plasma would be removed through his port-a-catheter, the "port-a-Cath" that had been a part of his body for the past three years.

On that first morning, his port-a-Cath was not working properly. The skilled technicians were becoming increasingly frustrated that they couldn't withdraw the necessary blood in the usual manner of this well-established procedure. They tried and tried and eventually asked Emilio to turn side to side, stand up, and move around to get the catheter moving. By now, he was devastated, as were we. He screamed and cried and squeezed our hands tightly.

One of the technicians had stepped away to call Dr. Guinan. When she arrived, she was troubled and seemingly frustrated. She said to her staff, "I am not upset with any of you. I am angry that this sophisticated and vital piece of equipment was not working properly for this frightened little boy and his parents." She held Emilio's hand and told him everything would be alright. She looked straight into my eyes and said, "I am determined to correct this situation and make things better for Emilio!"

I looked at her with a quizzical glance, gathered my words together, and in a frustrated tone, I said, "How is everything going to be better?"

Dr. Guinan regretfully told us that Emilio's port-a-Cath would have to be surgically removed and a new one inserted that evening. Mortified and unable to move, I screamed, "Two surgeries in one day!"

I had no idea how my little boy would endure such discomfort and pain once again.

Throughout Emilio's journey with cancer, the first time that I was paralyzed with fear was the day that he had his port-a-Cath put into his chest. That was the day of his diagnosis, March 28, 1998, two and a half years before THIS frighteningly unbelievable day. And this was only day one.

By the afternoon of September 3, we had already been in the hospital for five days. A few final rounds of chemotherapy and the start of radiation would take place before the transplant could begin. Doctors would harvest cells from Richard's bone marrow the following day. Richard told me that he was not the least bit nervous. After everything that Emilio had been through, Richard had absolutely no qualms about being Emilio's donor.

The three of us were napping in Emilio's room on Unit 6 West when Emilio's primary nurse, Abigail, entered with a warm meal for Emilio. Gratefully, he was hungry and happy to see her. Abigail always took the time to answer our questions and discuss what we could expect with each new day. She explained that Unit 6 West was one of the three most intensive units in the hospital. The other two were the Heart Transplant Unit and the ICU. Confidently,

Abigail said, "Only the most skilled pediatric oncology nurses could work in these units."

She continued to explain that these dedicated nurses cared for the same children living here for many months at a time. Abigail would be Emilio's primary nurse throughout his transplant and beyond. She told us, "Because I have worked in this unit for the past ten years, I have seen everything that could go wrong, and I have witnessed many miracles too." Of course, all I wanted to hear about were the miracles.

Abigail had plenty of miracle stories to share with us, and she never showed fear, no matter what Emilio was experiencing. She told my brother John that she was a believer in God, but when her time came to meet the dear Lord at the pearly gates, she would speak her mind. She told him, "How in the world could God allow children to get sick with cancer!"

Later that afternoon, we heard the cheers of people below our window. Glancing out the window, we saw a large group of people running. Nurse Abigail told us that the runners were training for the Boston Marathon that would take place the following spring.

Richard, who occasionally ran a few miles here and there, stood at the window watching them keenly. He suddenly turned to Emilio and said, "One day after we get out of here, the three of us will come back to Boston, and Daddy will run the Boston Marathon!"

Emilio declared, "Great Dad, I will run it with you!"

Richard did not know then that he would first need to qualify for the Boston Marathon. It would take him ten years to do so. Richard qualified just short of his 59th birthday and went on to run Boston three more times.

The love of a brother for his sister was never more profound than in those moments when John would walk into our hospital room. John, like my brother Michael, and our dad, was devoted to family. All three of these outstanding men were compassionate and loving and spent their lives dedicated to serving others in need.

Richard and I spent our honeymoon in Westport, Connecticut, seven years earlier, with John, his wife Nancy Jo Cappetta, and their first child, Johnny, who was only four months old.

It was a long six-hour commute from John's home to Boston and back again. For the first three weeks, John and Nancy Jo would come up every Saturday with their three children, Johnny, Matthew, and Chiara. Their youngest son, Rocco (our godson), had not yet been born.

Eventually, John would come to spend time with us on his own. Nancy Jo needed to be home, caring for the children. The visit was never an easy one for John to make. He worked hard and spent long hours working in Connecticut and sometimes in the New York office. With three small kids, he and Nancy Jo had so much to take care of on the weekends, yet he was always there.

Emilio loved his Uncle John and perked up every time he arrived on those late Saturday mornings. John wanted to give us breaks. He encouraged us to go outside, walk, visit a museum, or have a nice lunch.

An excerpt from John's email to our family in California~

"What you see in his room is a beautiful little boy fighting his pain and circumstances like a great war hero still on the battlefield. Under incredibly difficult circumstances, his countenance was steadfast determination. At times he exhaled audibly or gnashed his teeth to help him cope with his pain, but he would not give in to it. He rarely complained. On one occasion, when I was in his room, I heard him tell his mom to stop worrying about him so much."

Richard was so proud to be Emilio's donor. He was strong and fit mentally, spiritually, and physically. He considered it an honor and a privilege to help his son. Six ounces of bone marrow were harvested from Richard's body a few days before the transplant. When I asked Richard about the pain, he said, "Emilio has given me playful punches in the back that hurt more than having my bone marrow drawn."

Seven days into the transplant, Richard's Type 0 blood had transitioned into Emilio's body, and Emilio's previous blood type A changed to Type 0. Richard's marrow was grafting beautifully, and Emilio's cell count was rising. This was all good news, but Dr. Guinan reminded us of the challenges we could face as the transplant progressed; some organ failure was possible. Or, as Abigail reminded us, perhaps this wouldn't occur because she said, "Transplant miracles do happen."

Again, the game of Russian Roulette that we willingly signed up for was ready to begin. Emilio's first radiation treatment was scheduled for the following day. He had never been through radiation; it was not a part of his leukemia protocol. Emilio was brought into a room alone for his treatment. He had never been separated from us during treatment unless he was sedated for a procedure.

He was wide awake during radiation, sitting in a chair, crying. He could hear us, but he could not see us. Two very kind and patient radiologists were with him, trying to comfort him. We were seated in a separate room with a large screen that allowed us to see him. We read him a book and tried hard to comfort him with our words. We knew that he was scared and particularly struggling to find a way to see us. Our hearts were broken to see him suffering so much as he tried to find us.

Radiation therapy treats cancer by using high-energy waves to kill cancer cells. The goal is to destroy or damage cancer without hurting too many healthy cells.

The most common side effects of radiation are fatigue and skin changes, such as mouth sores. These symptoms started taking place within the first hour after Emilio's first 15-minute session.

Dr. Guinan walked into our hospital room as I was holding Emilio in my arms post-treatment. Emilio was nauseous and lethargic, lying quietly still with his eyes closed. He seemed so sad and scared. I was rocking him back and forth and thinking to myself, this is it. How can he possibly suffer more?

Dr. Guinan knew I was tormented. She joined me on the bed and softly draped one arm around my shoulder. She was carefully observing Emilio's face and the state of his discomfort. Deeply troubled, I said, "I know we cannot pack our bags, stop the transplant, and go home. If we could, I would do so right now. I am so afraid for Emilio."

With tears in her eyes, she held my hands and nodded her head. "Oh, Mrs. Nares," she said in her caring voice, "The challenge will be that Emilio's organs can get into trouble at any time. Radiation is new for him, and his little body has been through so much already from the three years of chemotherapy treatment and infections."

All I could do was reply with the question, "So this is Russian Roulette, right? Too much chemotherapy for too long a time can kill the good cells, not just the cancer cells, correct?"

"Correct," she replied, but let's focus now on the fact that "Emilio's white blood cells are rising, and Richard's healthy bone marrow has taken over within Emilio's system."

It was clear that all we could do was wait. We could not control the outcome or what would or would not happen within the coming weeks.

Upon admittance to the hospital, there was a section in the paperwork where we could add our religion of choice. Although Richard and I had not been practicing Catholics for many years, we surprised one another when we mutually wrote "Catholic" on the hospital form. I later said to him, "How interesting! Is it because once a Catholic, always a Catholic? Is it the comfort of our history? Or is it simply the safest place to land in this frightening, compromising position we find ourselves in?"

We settled on the answer of "familiarity," plain and simple.

The following morning, we found our answer. Writing the word "Catholic" led us straight to Sister Carlotta Gilarde, CSJ.

Sister Carlotta has served as one of the sisters of St. Joseph of Boston for more than 65 years. Sister served as a bilingual chaplain in San Ricardo Parish in Peru for 27 years. She was the first bi-lingual chaplain at Boston Children's Hospital. We loved Sister Carlotta immediately. Although she is tiny, Sister is filled with dynamic energy, courage, and determination.

The three of us were joined at the hip every day while Emilio was in the hospital. She often told me that she loved being a presence to the families at all hours of the day. When Sister Carlotta had a particularly difficult day visiting sick children and their moms and dads, she would sometimes say to me, "Oh Diane, I ask God every evening, why? Why must children suffer? My beloved God, for what reason or lesson could there possibly be to justify the sobering reality of children living with cancer?" She was so distraught because although she was deeply religious, she couldn't understand this kind of suffering. It made no sense to her at all.

I was relieved to learn that it wasn't just me who couldn't understand how God would allow this to happen. Even a dedicated nun saw it as a senseless, unnecessary act of torture.

Sister Carlotta's presence during those excruciatingly painful days brought me a tremendous sense of comfort. The day was made a little easier every time I heard her sweet and loving voice outside of our room as she spoke the words, "Diane, Richard, would you like to pray together?"

We would answer in unison, "Oh yes, Sister, thank you, our day will be a little bit brighter since you are with us." She would humbly smile and begin her comforting prayers.

Being in the middle of a bone marrow transplant with my only child was like swimming laps and never finding the end of the pool. August 30 through October 15, were endless days and nights filled with debilitating fear. Once again, having control over the situations that we encountered every day in Unit 6 West was beyond our reach.

Chapter 21
Angels in the Hallway

The summer heat had departed, and the late September fall was beginning to chill the evenings. It was a Thursday and my turn to spend the night with Emilio. Since day one, Richard and I had established a routine. We both are people who desperately need a sense of order in our lives.

We alternated nights sleeping in the hospital with Emilio. The one who slept at the hospital was awakened sporadically throughout the night. Nurses would come in and go out, as the IV pumps would chime and ring depending on what chemo was needed and when it was needed. It was this way all night long.

The parent who slept at the Ronald McDonald House was the one who got uninterrupted sleep, although stress and worry never ceased, and we still ended up having sleepless nights even in the toasty comfort of the secluded room in The House.

Any way you looked at it, the whole routine was a vicious cycle but a cycle that we needed to cling to as we navigated our way through that extremely dysfunctional time in our lives.

On a Thursday evening, I arrived back at the hospital early to relieve Richard. While I was doing laundry at The

House, he called to tell me Emilio was having a particularly difficult day. He told me that he and Emilio had spent most of the day rallying back and forth with a cold cloth compress. By now, Emilio was in various degrees of discomfort most days. For the first time in his three years of treatment, he was now experiencing bed sores, extreme itching, intermittent fevers, and overall anger and frustration with his relentless situation.

Nurse Abigail told Richard that pressing cold washcloths on Emilio's forehead would ease some pain. There were no naps that day. Emilio would get angry but would never cry.

"All day long, Emilio would get mad as hell every time I tried to lay a cloth on his forehead. The minute I got close to his face, Emilio would take the cloth and throw it against the wall," Richard said.

"He was mad, Diane," he continued. "I have never seen him like this before. Whenever I took a bundle of towels and kept trying to get them close to his head, Emilio would throw a fit."

This routine went on that afternoon for almost three hours until Emilio finally closed his eyes and fell asleep from profound exhaustion.

After Richard's next turn to stay with Emilio, he told me the following morning that when it was time for the two of them to go to sleep, he heard Emilio whisper, "I love you, Dad." Richard responded with the words, "I love you, Emilio." Seconds later, Richard heard Emilio repeating his words, "I love you, Dad." And so, the repetition of these precious words continued throughout the night until the wee hours of the morning.

This story prompted me to say to Richard, "Get dressed and go down to Au Bon Pain, order the biggest cup of coffee and chocolate croissant that they have, take it out to the healing gardens, and enjoy yourself while you can. I suspect we are in for some rocky nights ahead with minimal sleep!"

Gratefully, Richard listened, and an hour later, he headed back on foot to the Ronald McDonald House for some well-needed sleep. It was my turn now to experience whatever adventures Emilio had in mind. The truth is, poor little guy, how could he possibly know how he would feel each day? It depended on the particular medicine and treatment plan. Some days were better than others.

I took a break that afternoon and went to the Isabella Gardner Museum. The walk over felt good on Boston's warm but very fall-like day. Richard and I managed to get out each day for a brief walk, sometimes together and sometimes solo.

At home, we lived a very active lifestyle with a structured exercise routine, but here in Boston, living in and out of the hospital had taken a toll on our bodies. Our muscles and joints hurt. We needed physical and mental movement to endure this new, unwelcome, challenging lifestyle that the three of us had been hurled into without our approval. We needed to feel the sun on our faces. Even when we were solo, the solitude was a welcomed distraction.

It felt normal and sane to remove oneself from the constant buzzing of the IV poles and the bags filled with chemo. There is only so much that a parent can take as they watch poison filter into their child's body—life-saving poison, but nevertheless, terrifying to think about. The walk to the museum was a much-needed distraction.

I returned later to Emilio's room to persuade Richard to join me downstairs at Au Bon Pain for a healthy and delicious early dinner. After hearing Richard's stories about his two challenging overnights this week, I knew I was in for another rollercoaster ride with minimal sleep. A dinner break with Richard seemed like a lovely finish to a somewhat peaceful day. We both said simultaneously, "The calm before the storm is upon us."

The grilled chicken, rosemary potatoes, and maple-induced Brussel sprouts were delicious, minus our usual glass of wine with dinner. Since arriving in Boston, we had not partaken in enjoying a glass of wine with dinner. We mutually agreed that we would not be able to tolerate any substance that could alter our mental state. We needed to stay sharp and clear in our thoughts as best as possible. Anything could change Emilio's health at any given moment, throwing us off our game. We could not afford an altered mind, body, or soul. We could control not consuming alcohol, but sleep deprivation was another matter. This was out of our control.

After dinner, we returned to Emilio's room. The two of us settled in with some movies and a handful of his evening medicines. Richard kissed us both goodnight and made his way to the elevator that would take him to the bottom floor and out into the cool evening air that would guide him back to the Ronald McDonald House to sleep. The morning watch soon would begin again for Richard, along with the rising sun of another frightening day in Unit 6 West.

That night the nurse on duty was Lynn Philips, one of Emilio's favorites. I was grateful to all of the Boston nurses in the transplant unit; everyone was loving, compassionate, and knew how to talk to Emilio, especially as the days wore on and his various levels of pain deepened.

Nurse Lynn was on duty the previous week when Emilio's drawings started changing in style. He went from drawing the three of us holding hands in Boston Commons, with a pastel palette of colors, to a dark, black crayon that revealed a hollow face with sunken cheeks and eyes. He had colored a blue mouth with a turned-down smile.

"This is me, Mommy," Emilio said, "Just like daddy's Van Gogh picture in the museum." Nurse Lynn showed it to me that evening and explained that this often happened to the older kids. I was so scared that something like this was ahead for Emilio. He was almost six years old, and everything about enduring his cancer was beginning to change for him. He was filled with questions and, most often, anger. He often said, "Why am I bald, Mommy? Everything hurts!"

One evening Emilio insisted that we call his friend Michael in San Diego. "Please, Mommy, I need to talk to Michael. Please call him," he said. The three-hour time difference was so difficult. It was most often 11:00 p.m. on the West Coast when Emilio would cry out these words. We couldn't make this call at such a late time for a six-year-old and his parents. I tried hard to calm Emilio down, "Sweetheart, we need to wait until morning. I promise we will call Michael tomorrow, and he will be rested and so excited to talk to you."

When Emilio got like this, it was hard to talk him down. He cried for an hour that particular evening. It broke my heart. My pain was particularly excruciating emotionally because I could no longer comfort my little boy. Every day was becoming more and more unbearable. Emilio's life was one of ravaging chemotherapy side effects, pain, bedsores, mouth sores, and steroid-induced misery.

That evening, October 1, 2000, summer was turning into the cold chill of a new season. Fall was upon us and the color of the leaves on the trees was turning into vibrant orange and yellow hues that we had only seen in books or movies but had never seen in person.

At some point around 2:00 a.m. Emilio was having difficulty breathing. He was up and down continuously for what seemed to be a very long and laborious hour. Lynn and I took turns keeping the oxygen mask on his face. Barely able to stay awake, I remember dozing off as Lynn got Emilio to calm down and sleep a bit.

Within moments, without warning, eight members of the Code Blue Team stormed into Emilio's room and immediately began to intubate him. I had not been aware that they had been on-call all night long in case Emilio got into trouble.

Hearing them storm in, I shot up out of my chair, rushing to get to Emilio's bed. I held him tightly and kissed his face for what seemed to be only a few seconds. One of the nurses on duty called Richard and told him to return to the hospital as soon as possible.

When Richard and I alternated sleeping arrangements, the one at The House always held on to fear that a call could come in the middle of the night that would tell us Emilio was in trouble. We never truly rested or slept well at The House, even though the comfort level was so high.

Richard was always prepared when it was his turn to sleep at The House. On that particular fall night, his winter coat and boots were by his bedside. The 2:00 a.m. call woke him up from the deep sleep that had finally embraced his body shortly after midnight.

Richard got dressed quickly, grabbed his coat, and dashed out the front door of the quiet Victorian House that had offered respite to us for the previous 30 days.

He wildly ran like a madman to a destination point where he had no idea what he would find there.

As Richard entered the revolving front door, he zoomed right past the security guard. It was customary to stop at the front security station, announce oneself, and check in. The guard chased Richard up the many stairs until Richard turned around and said, "I need to get to my son. He is in trouble in the Bone Marrow Transplant Unit." The guard quickly guided Richard to the closest elevator and personally escorted him to the unit.

When Richard approached Emilio's hospital room door, he heard some people mumbling and understood only a few of the words they were speaking. One of them said to the others, "He has stopped breathing." Richard stood motionless as he found himself unable to enter the room. The entire Bone Marrow Transplant Team and the eight members of the Code Blue Team were examining Emilio just prior to his intubation. I was tucked away next to Emilio, holding on to his one available hand while his other hand was bandaged close to his body with various tubes attached. Within 30 seconds tops, Emilio was breathing again as Richard raced to his bedside. Richard reached out and touched him just seconds before Emilio was being wheeled straight to the elevator and down to the bottom floor, where the ICU doctor and nurse were waiting for him.

Rosa was with us the entire week leading up to these devastating early morning hours. Rosa clearly made an impression in her short time in the hospital unit. The nurses referred to her as "Emilio's second mama."

A caring hospital staff member set up a cot for her in the back room of the hospital cafeteria. Someone called Rosa's cell phone, just in time for her to race back up to Emilio's room before he was taken to ICU. She stood next to Richard and me in Emilio's new hospital room.

The ICU doctor explained to us what an induced coma was and why it had occurred. We would still be able to feel Emilio's hands squeeze our hands, and he could hear us speak to him. As grim as the situation was, hearing the doctor's words reassured me.

Once again, we felt hopeful when Dr. Guinan arrived that morning at 6:00 a.m. She had come to explain to us that the transplant would continue and Emilio would have a chance to rest from the trauma. She and her team were keeping a very close eye on him at all times.

We slept by his side the rest of the morning, often waking as every disease specialist visited his room within the following 24 hours. We were introduced to the Infectious Disease Team, the Pulmonary specialist, and the Kidney and Liver hospital specialists—each with their own teams who examined Emilio daily. All this attention occurred while he was safe, and we hoped to sleep peacefully.

We were soon to find out that since Boston Children's Hospital was one of the best teaching institutions in the country, a variety of young men and women at their Residency level would be observing the various specialists who cared for Emilio. These bright, young, soon-to-be doctors had chosen Pediatric Oncology as their life-long specialty. As we met each one of them, I quietly muttered to Richard, "Why? How can they do this?" Richard gently responded, "Why and how can we do this?" It took me a few seconds to get the words out, "They chose to do this. We didn't." He nodded with a look in his eyes that reflected a painful reality check.

All other details of that "middle of the night horror show" that preceded these two weeks in the ICU are muffled in my memory. I do not know how many hours Emilio's breathing was in danger. I asked myself repeatedly, did Nurse Lynn call the Code Blue Team early enough? How did they know exactly when to storm into his room?

We began to understand more after Dr. Guinan took over communications early that morning when Emilio settled into the ICU. She explained Emilio needed to be intubated so that a medically induced coma could occur, which would put him in a safe place to get oxygen to his brain. She continued to explain that Emilio would not be able to speak in a medically induced coma, and his eyes would be closed. She compared his situation to one of sleeping peacefully. She assured us that Emilio could hear the sounds in the environment, such as our footsteps and our movements around him. He could also hear our voices and feel the squeeze from our hands.

The only moment I felt any sense of comfort was when Emilio returned my squeezes. My hand trembled as I felt his little fingers wrap around mine. He held my hand tightly as if he couldn't let me go. Suddenly I could breathe again.

Richard and I moved into the hotel directly across the street from Children's Hospital, where we had spent our first night with Emilio. We needed to be very close by in case of an emergency. Our large room at the Ronald McDonald House would still be there for us when Emilio woke up. We would all return to The House, where his favorite toys, books, stuffed animals, and videos lived.

Emilio remained in the same condition for two weeks until one morning, Sunday, October 15, he stopped returning my hand squeezes.

The call came as we were still sleeping. The voice on the other end of the phone was that of Dr. Powers, who was on duty. She softly said, "Mr. and Mrs. Nares, it would be a good idea if you came to the unit now. We will explain when you get here."

There was little to do but splash water on our faces and brush our teeth. We had the foresight to put on our sweaters because it was early morning, still dark outside, and the warm summer weather had almost overnight turned into a cool October breeze.

We quickly made our way across Longwood Avenue, which took us directly to the front entrance of Boston Children's Hospital.

When we arrived in Emilio's ICU room, it was 6:30 a.m., and we found it very strange to see both Sister Carlotta and Dr. Guinan sitting in chairs next to Emilio's bedside.

They both held our hands as tears streamed down their cheeks.

Dr. Guinan had spoken to us often about the possibility of organ failure happening during a transplant of any sort. Emilio's body was in such a compromised situation. His lungs and kidneys were now in trouble. She softly said, "Richard, Diane, I am so sorry, but Emilio's situation is getting worse. There is nothing more that we can do to improve the course of action that his body is taking." Once again, that familiar feeling of deep grief crippled my legs as I fell to the floor.

As Richard lifted me up, Dr. Guinan sadly continued to speak her words, "Emilio's little body has taken on so much more than could ever have been expected, too much chemo, too many infections, over too long a period of time."

We had tried the last option on this crippling journey. There was nothing else to do. Sister Carlotta joined the doctor to explain how these last hours of Emilio's life could look if we agreed. We had no questions left to ask. We had no energy between the two of us to come up with a clever idea that might turn around these horrifying words or hopeless moments.

We knew it was time to let him go.

Dr. Guinan explained, "We will transfer Emilio to a small private room in the ICU. The two of you can lay in bed with him for as long as you wish. All of Emilio's tubes will be removed. He will continue to breathe on his own for at least the next five to six hours."

During those hours, we held Emilio in our arms. At some point, the hospital priest, Father McNamara, came into the room to administer last rites to Emilio. Sister Carlotta joined him, and the four of us silently prayed.

Father McNamara and Sister Carlotta slowly removed themselves from the room. I remember that for one moment, I thought how sad it was that Rosa had to return to San Diego the day before. She did not have this opportunity to hold Emilio one last time.

As the hour of 3:00 p.m. approached, Emilio took his final breaths.

I knelt over my precious son and held him tightly in my arms. A tremendous force soon surrounded the three of us. It was "tremendous" because it was an overwhelming, intense awareness of love and understanding. Following the ceasing of his final breath, another mysterious phenomenon occurred.

Although the feeling was brief, I felt no sorrow but a blissful sense of peace. I knew in those moments that Emilio would always be with me. I felt a powerful, grand energy slip out of his body as it settled into the space between the three of us. Then a bright light highlighted Emilio's limp body. A light that had been waiting to receive Emilio's sacred soul and carry him away with force so grand, there were no more thoughts or words that could explain those moments of truth.

That momentary lack of sorrow quickly shifted to excruciating pain as we attempted to speak to one another about the revelation that had just occurred. The words could not come out of our mouths. We had both found ourselves stooped forward with our heads lying motionless in our hands. Suddenly the door opened, and Dr. Guinan and Sister Carlotta walked in.

These two loving, compassionate souls had cared deeply for the three of us for the past two and a half months. Each one of them, eyes filled with tears, told us to stay and hold Emilio for as long as we wanted.

I don't remember when we decided to relinquish holding Emilio's body, but it soon became apparent we had nothing more to give.

Sister Carlotta guided us out of the room and handed us right into the arms of John and Nancy Jo. They were waiting most of the day in the ICU lobby. They came to take care of us and help us do whatever we needed or wanted to do.

We didn't know that Sister Carlotta had called John that morning. I was so grateful when John told me that he and Nancy Jo had come into the room earlier in the afternoon to kiss Emilio and say goodbye to him. I didn't even know that they had done so.

The four of us walked out of the hospital that chilly fall afternoon. John and Nancy Jo made sure that we had food available, although we had no appetites and couldn't have swallowed anything had we been hungry. We could barely breathe.

I vaguely remember sleeping in the hotel room as the two of them went to stay in our room at the Ronald McDonald House. Their intention was not just to have a place to sleep that night but to take on the hugely important job of packing the "big black suitcase" with all Emilio's favorite things.

I don't know how the two of them could get into their car the next day and drive back to Connecticut, having spent a sleepless night and a day filled with grief and devastation. We will never forget the compassion, familial love, and selfless actions that John and Nancy Jo bestowed upon us on that dreadful day and those excruciating painful months that preceded it.

Chapter 22
Home Without Emilio

The next morning John and Nancy Jo coordinated with Richard's brother, Charlie, back in San Diego to get Emilio's body on a flight to the mortuary in San Diego. They also spent significant hours getting us an outbound flight home.

The only words we could speak that morning was, "We want to go home now. We must be home when Emilio gets there!"

On their way home to Connecticut, John and Nancy Jo drove us to Boston Logan Airport. The four of us bought Starbucks coffees and waited in line to get our tickets to fly to Philadelphia, the only outbound flight that could eventually get us to San Diego.

As we approached the agent in Philadelphia to purchase tickets to San Diego, the agent told us that the plane was full and there were no other flights until evening.

Richard leaned in, and with a face filled with stress and sorrow, he told the agent, "We need to get on that flight now! Our son is in a coffin on an outbound flight from Boston; we must get home before he does!"

We were both sobbing as the ticket agent's face turned the color of ash. He quickly printed tickets and passed us through the gate. A security guard held onto our shoulders, as once again, we were visibly weakened by the trauma of our entire experience the day before.

I felt a moment of relief as it was apparent these two airline employees were sensitive enough to see we were fragile and distraught in our quest to get home before our son's dead body arrived.

I remember little about that six-hour flight home. I couldn't eat a morsel of food served, and I could not drink any water unless I drank it through a straw. My lips were parched, and I could feel my skin turning cold, pale, and clammy. The long flight made me weary and uncomfortable.

Several hours into the flight, I heard a voice from a familiar-looking face standing next to me in the aisle. "Hi, Diane!" a woman's voice shouted in a high-pitched tone. I recognized her as one of the young cocktail waitresses who worked with me in my first restaurant management position a lifetime ago.

I must have looked at her as if I had seen a ghost because she paused for a moment and then quickly moved along as if she had realized that I was either incredibly sick or had no idea who she was.

Chapter 23
And Then There Were Two

I don't recall who picked us up at the airport and drove us home.

What I do remember is that an entourage of my closest friends and family were waiting for us on the front porch with Sierra. They were holding on tightly, with tears streaming down their cheeks, to an extremely tall banner, with the words "Welcome Home" wrapped around an array of hearts. My sisters, Nancy, Teresa, and Patty held onto Sierra tightly. Upon seeing us pull up to the curb, she tried to make a mad dash out the front gate. My sister-in-law Roberta had come to clean our house.

As Patty told me later, "Roberta worked quietly and diligently for several hours in order to make the house beautiful before your return." That day, my muddled mind and inability to function made it impossible for me to remember such acts of kindness for a very long time. I will always be grateful for the love and compassion my friends and family showed Richard and me at such an excruciatingly painful time.

My close friend Marti had taken Sierra to the groomer. She was beautifully clean, smelled like lavender, and wore a bright, tomato-red scarf around her neck. Sierra ran down the front porch stairs to greet us. She was sniffing the ground and circling around us. We knew that she was looking for Emilio. Her "pack" as she knew it, was missing someone significant. Once back inside the house, she paced and panted up and down the hallway in search of him.

Sierra waited for Emilio on his bedroom floor for the following two weeks. Someone later told us that we could have taken her to the mortuary to see his body and smell him for one final time. We had no idea that animals had a peaceful acceptance of death as long as they had this opportunity for closure.

Just like Sierra, we were looking for him everywhere in those first few days.

Where was he? The absence of Emilio in our home resulted in an unbearable first evening without him. Thank God for proper sleeping aids in the form of a little pill which ultimately allowed us to find some slumber on the hard edge of darkness.

The first morning was the worst. We awoke and realized we would never again hear Emilio's footsteps racing down the hallway. I turned to Richard and said, "How can we possibly get through this first day without him?" Richard was the first to say the words that were already laying and waiting on the tip of my tongue to release.

Carefully and hesitating for only a moment, he said, "All I want to do is die and crawl into the grave with Emilio." Gasping for breath, I answered, "That's exactly how I feel."

Somehow, we got out of bed and walked down the hallway, looking for Sierra. She had been sitting at the front door, waiting for Emilio to come home. She ran to our feet and pushed herself against my leg, begging me to take her for a walk. We had to move against all desires to open the front door and encounter the world. She needed to go outside. She needed to be fed. She needed her family. Sierra was our responsibility, and we reluctantly re-entered life.

We still wanted to die on that first morning without Emilio, but we knew we could not. He would want us to take care of his dog.

Those excruciatingly difficult moments were the moments when I learned that grief doesn't unfold in an orderly fashion. Grief is chaotic. It's messy. I need order in my life, and that just isn't always possible when one is grieving. What I didn't yet know was that grief changes all the time. I eventually learned that our love, Richard and mine, would get us through the darkest moments of our lives.

We got up and out of bed that morning and every morning that followed. We had been on a cancer journey for the past three years. Now we were on the journey of grief. An unbearable journey that we knew nothing about until we found ourselves in the thick of it. All that we were capable of doing was to put one foot in front of the other so that we could get out the door and walk our dog.

Early one morning that followed, I woke up and found myself sleeping in Emilio's bed. My head was squished into his pillow as I breathed in his scent. I was waiting for him to come back and jump into bed with me. His sweet smell was everywhere, in every drawer, shelf, and child's book that I opened. Where was he? As I buried my head further into his bright red comforter, I opened my eyes to see Sierra staring at me. She placed her little paw right on my left leg and continued to sit by my side. Sierra sat so still. I knew she was also waiting for him to come home.

Richard walked in to find me holding tightly onto one of Emilio's flannel pajama tops. He crawled into Emilio's bed with me. We couldn't let go of the pajama top until it was soaking wet from our tears.

The next morning, I shared this story with my sister Patty. "Oh, Patty," I cried out to her, "How will I ever make it through Emilio's Memorial Service on Friday?" Patty replied, "We should get you a sedative to take that day." I did not want to take a med that might make me unaware of how I was feeling. I suspected I would be numb with shock, which might be enough to help get me through the day. I wanted to be myself no matter how tortuous it would be. I told her no, thank you, and she asked me what it felt like to wake up every day without Emilio. The only response I could give her was, "Sad, I feel very, very sad."

That became the only word that I could use for months to come. I was hopelessly sad for a very long time.

Our family and close friends made all the arrangements for the day of Emilio's service. Early that morning, several construction workers gathered in the street in front of our house and started picking up the red cones at the curb placed there the previous evening. They were scheduled to start working on the water pipes that morning.

With coffee in hand, Richard headed to the street curb to see what was happening. An older gentleman who appeared to be the lead worker on the job told Richard that he had received a call from the city to cease working on the pipes in front of our house on Fort Stockton Drive.

He said, "Mr. Nares, on behalf of the City of San Diego, we offer our condolences on the loss of your son, and we acknowledge the difficult day that lies ahead for you and your wife." With their heads held low to the ground, the crew quietly removed the workload and headed off to another block.

Richard's brother Charlie and his wife, Sally, picked us up, and the four of us drove silently the entire thirty minutes to Encinitas. What could we say? I had no idea whether or not I would be able to speak with anyone.

I later found the eulogy that my brother John had written and presented at Emilio's memorial service. I couldn't even hear these beautiful words that morning. Grief clouded my senses. Here is an excerpt:

"They did not look at parenthood as an inevitable step in their life plan. Something one simply does when they reach a certain age. When they had Emilio, they said to each other, they said to all of us, they said to God, 'Wow! We cannot believe God has given US this incredible gift. Every single day was an incredible gift from God!' They had 2,108 incredible days. 2,108 such divine gifts. They cherished each and every one of those days. This is how they loved their son."

Emilio's ten cousins on my side of the family wrote a poem to Emilio, honoring his life and vowing never to forget him. I became overwhelmed with grief as I listened to my niece Giovanna read their poetry. It was equally surreal as all ten children lined up on the altar in front of the huge crowd that graced the pews of the Encinitas Self Realization Fellowship Church. A group of individuals came to pay their respects and mourn the loss of Emilio's life.

Gia read the poem beautifully, and all of the children managed to stand together in solidarity through what would become a few of the most difficult moments they would experience in their lifetime. A few of them were probably too young to remember, but the older ones told me many years later that they never forgot the experience of saying a final goodbye to their little cousin whom they loved so much. I could have never known then how much the passing of time would deepen my love for these beautiful children and how much I would need each of them in my life.

Thank you, Jordan, JJ, Sean, Caitlin, Gia, Danielle, Jon Rocco, Johnny, Matthew, Chiara, and Rocco. And the gifts of love that came to us always from our Nares and Anderson's nieces and nephews Jim, Jill, Brent, Andrea, and Charlie Jr.

Over 300 people attended Emilio's memorial service including community leaders and media professionals. Several TV and radio news stations came with cameras, and the monks had to usher them out of the church and into the patio garden so they would not disturb this sacred service.

Emilio's story of searching and never finding a marrow donor for two years encouraged thousands of people to join the bone marrow registry. Throughout his journey, his story continued to be told in the hopes of saving the lives of anyone who needed a bone marrow transplant. Emilio inspired hundreds of people in our community and across the country.

It would take me years before I could have the generosity of thought to realize how difficult it must have been for our entire family to endure the loss of their little nephew, their precious cousin. The thought of how our parents, Emilio's grandparents, must have felt haunts me now.

Their babies had lost their only baby. I now know their despair was as deep as ours.

Richard's mother, Dancy, had passed away when Emilio was four months old, but his dad and my mom and dad had watched Emilio grow from a newborn baby to a toddler to a little boy ready for kindergarten. Their hearts were broken.

I will never forget a particular day two months after Emilio's service. It was the week before Christmas when I visited my mom and dad. My dad greeted me at the door, and for a few seconds, he glanced around, then said, "Hey honey, where's Emilio?"

"Oh, Daddy," I said, "remember Emilio is no longer with us."

He looked confused, then softly said, "Oh yes, that's right, I am so sorry, now I remember."

My brilliant father, Rocco Michael Cappetta, had been diagnosed two years prior with Alzheimer's disease. He was 78 years old. My father died on January 22, 2001, three months after his little grandson had left this world. I loved my father beyond what words could describe. He had been my closest confidant throughout my childhood and my young adulthood. To my complete surprise and dismay, I could not grieve my father's death. I simply did not have it in me to do so. My loss of Emilio had taken every ounce of emotion out of me. I had nothing more to give.

I thought that perhaps if my father had died from cancer or an accident, I might have felt a deeper level of sadness. The reality that Alzheimer's disease was slowly taking away my brilliant father's mind was a red flag that something far worse would soon happen. I just wanted my dad to have some sense of relief. I knew that science had not yet found a way to reverse Alzheimer's.

I felt like I lost my dad three years prior when I began to notice that he was slipping away from us. Apart from my inability to grieve him properly, I prayed that God would save him from the more difficult symptoms that would surely come. I feared that my mother would suffer greatly and that her frail body would never be able to care for my father when his disease progressed into that commonplace of anger that so many Alzheimer's patients eventually experienced. If he had walked out the door and lost his way home, my mother would not be able to find him. Mary was in a wheelchair by this time, and I knew she was scared to death at what the future might hold for her and my dad.

By the time of Rocco's death, his quick mind and brilliant words had been slipping away from him, and he was losing control of his short-term memory. Sadly, we watched our dad forget most of the actions of his particular days, as each day fell into the next one until he took his final breath and finally found peace. Rocco was the finest of men, one of the brightest, and a saint on earth. I found it much easier to smile when I thought of his kind face than to cry. I was blessed with the greatest dad.

It would take three years after my father's death for me to finally grieve my loss of him. One early summer morning, I woke up from an incredibly vivid dream.

My dad and I were walking on the beach as we had done so many times since I was a little girl, and then years later when I had become a young, independent woman. We were having one of our long intellectual and spiritual conversations. I woke up sobbing, knowing that I was finally desperately missing him. I needed him here to comfort me through my continued grief over the loss of Emilio. Rocco had always been my sounding board. Choking on my tears, I finally felt the sadness of the loss of my beloved father. His absence from my life became a profound reality. I was slightly comforted to realize that I could feel again.

On the day of Emilio's service, a reception line formed on the patio behind the church following the service. Childhood friends drove down from Los Angeles, and others flew in from out of state. Industry friends of mine showed up to offer us their love and condolences.

Rosa came with her husband, Eduardo. Rosa and I hugged one another; we did not want to let go. She was always Emilio's mama too. He loved her deeply. She grieved for him, as I did.

Rosa's daughter Rosita was like a sister to Emilio. They loved one another immensely. Rosita was five years old when Emilio was born. Her heart was broken when Emilio died. Years later, after Rosita graduated from college, she wrote me a letter that Rosa brought me on one of her many visits. It took me a couple of days to read it because I knew that the moment I did so, I would not be able to stop crying.

Here is an excerpt from Rosita's letter:

"My life changed completely not only when Emilio passed away but when he was born. Emilio changed the heart of everybody in my family. Life continues, but Emilio is always here with us. I was so motivated by what I experienced with Emilio that I chose to go to college and study psychology. Today I offer my services at a Tijuana hospital. When I walk through those doors every morning, the minute they open, I think about everything Emilio went through and what families experience. I put in a lot of overtime and extra hours talking to patients and families, and my colleagues question me, 'Why are you still here?' It's not wasting time. It's Emilio's gift transferred through me. Emilio was not upset with life. He loved life, so now I can give back what I learned from him. Every time I do something, I do it in the name of my 'little brother'."

After about 20 minutes in the receiving line, Richard and I glanced at one another, knowing that the grief was just too unbearable for us to handle. We knew that we had to leave. We had to get to Richard's brother Gilbert's beach house, where a reception would be held after the service. The same place we were married on the patio deck with our family and closest friends, seven years prior, in 1993.

We hoped we could breathe again at Gilbert's house.

The familiar smell of the ocean provided relief, but soon I felt chilled and weak. I turned to Richard and told him that I wanted to go home. I had underestimated the magnitude of the effort required to speak with loved ones. Sitting here for even one more moment was beyond human strength. I was eternally grateful to everyone who worked hard to give Emilio a proper day of remembrance. It was their time to act heroically.

I just couldn't bear another moment awake. Perhaps I should have taken that sedative.

Chapter 24
Throwing It All Away

The following morning, with a burst of energy like a mad woman, I threw away all the things that had previously been deemed "essential."

I filled trash bags with left-over medicines, every syringe, and portable IV tube Emilio needed for the past three years to survive. All signs of his cancer treatment were tossed out of my sight in a ferocious, aggressive manner that surprised me.

for a few brief moments, I felt in control of my life again until a wave of exhaustion began to drain me. I just woke up; how could I already be so tired? I asked myself this question repeatedly.

I desperately wanted to join Emilio. I tried to open the grave as you would a book and slip right in, next to his side, holding his hand. I had no concept of how grief would get in the way of every move I made. All I was looking for was some peace, some respite. My desire to no longer want to live was an acceptable response to a disappearance that every part of me refused to accept.

I knew I had some serious grief work to do, but I would first have to rest. The fatigue was overbearing. I was constantly thinking about how wrong it was that Emilio

196

died. He died so young; he was so beautiful. Dying at five years old is not the proper order of life. The mystery of this truth was impenetrable.

Just because I decided to join the living instead of dying didn't mean I was ready to do the work. Just because I had always been determined to succeed didn't mean that I would naturally accept grief into my life and conquer it. There is no such thing as conquering grief. I felt as if I was in a perpetual state of choking. Every step I took soon swallowed me up into a nightmare of despair.

Exactly two months after Emilio's passing, a dear friend stopped by the house with a gift. Sara Menendez has had her share of loss and grief. Her beloved husband, Miquel, died in a car accident three weeks after their wedding day. Sara is a compassionate, generous friend who continues to lovingly be a part of my life.

Sara told me that morning, December 15, 2000, "Diane, this gift is not for you to pay bills. This gift is for you and Richard to go somewhere and surround yourselves with beauty as you begin taking baby steps toward healing and recovery."

There was only one place we could think of that might provide some moments of comfort. That place was Big Sur. With Sara's gift, we checked into the Ventana Inn & Spa. The redwood trees and the Pacific Ocean surrounded us. Big Sur is a place where we could feel tiny amongst the glory of nature.

Our history in Big Sur began with the coastal painting trip when we were first married. Emilio joined us on two trips to Big Sur, first when he was ten months old and later when he was two years old.

We were so grateful to Sara that we could return to this place of such comfort, but we couldn't have imagined how deep the sorrow would be to experience the grandeur of this sacred place we had shared with our little boy just three years ago before this visit. On this trip, we returned without him, and the pain was unbearable.

Although the beauty of Big Sur surrounded us at every turn, the sea, the deer at sunrise, and even the yoga retreat in the redwoods could not reduce the intensity of my sorrow. It had been only two months without Emilio in my daily life. What was I thinking? Did I really believe that any place or anyone could reduce my pain?

I was getting used to the unwanted phlegm that got stuck in my throat every time I took a breath. Is this what my life will be like forever?

A few bites of food would be all that I could swallow. I began eating sporadically because the hunger was so profound, but consuming small bites would make me full. Breathing and eating no longer paralleled one another. It was one or the other.

In the many grief books that I tried to read; the phrase "God's Anesthesia" showed up several times in reference to how to survive the first couple of months after the death of your loved one. These two words represent a sheer but profoundly strengthening shield surrounding the body and mind, helping us get through the initial agonizing moments of grief. Our loved one's funeral, for example, or how to possibly answer endless questions such as; How are you feeling? What can I do to help you, or the worst statement that anyone can ever say, "Emilio is in a better place."

What does this mean? Experience taught me that this is a statement someone makes when they have no idea what to say. Well, they should just shut up and say nothing. When I first heard these words, I desperately wanted to shout back, "Here with me is the only place where Emilio should be. There is no better place!" In the first three months after Emilio died, I was angry most of the time. I hid it well. It was easier to do, than to find myself lashing out at others.

I returned to work right about that time. It was the start of a brand-new year, January 3, 2001.

The entire management team in my company was incredibly compassionate and patient with me. They had never had an employee whose child had died. The HR handbooks didn't provide insight into how to act with me or what the right words to say to me were. They took a step back and allowed me to come to them when I wanted.

I put on my boxing gloves every morning and returned to the world of selling wine and managing my teams. Almost everyone was gentle and quiet with me. I didn't want to talk about my loss or my pain. Instinctually I knew that I would never make it through the day if I started to do so. Instead, I thanked them for their embrace or their words of sorrow. I did my job, but "God's Anesthesia" was definitely beginning to wear off, and I suddenly felt much more vulnerable. Returning to work meant I had to surround myself with people and venture out. I was about to embark on a crash course in learning to survive amidst the avalanche of grief.

A few weeks after I returned to work, I found myself standing in an aisle of an upscale-wine shop in San Diego, hoping to see the owner or his wife, whom I knew well. I planned to get this encounter over with quickly. They had been great friends over the years, and I knew they were crushed at my loss of Emilio.

One of the clerks told me they both had to drive up to LA for business but that I would be in good hands with their new manager. His name escapes me now, but as the manager approached, he said, "I've heard everything about you, Diane, and I am sorry for your loss. My father is a pediatric oncologist, and he wants to know why Emilio died when the success rate for ALL leukemia is so high?"

My first reaction was one of shock. How could he ever ask me such a question?

I wanted desperately to have the strength to dispute this question, but I suddenly found myself unable to move my legs. All I wanted to do was run out the front door, and I did.

He followed me outside and mumbled an apology of sorts as I finally found my sea legs and dashed toward my car.

Sequestered inside my car, I knew I could not drive or even pull out of the parking lot. I leaned against my car door and started sobbing uncontrollably. I called my friend Genevieve who also worked in the wine industry. Attempting to tell her what had happened, all I could muster up was a sobbing voice declaring my need for her to rescue me!

Genevieve immediately said, "Stay inside your car, turn on some music, and don't try to leave. I will be there in 20 minutes."

I sat motionless while I asked myself a myriad of questions. What kept coming up was, "How can I possibly do this kind of work? Everything about my job is social, it's happy, it's all about wine and food, and here I sit, unable to get out of my car! How many years will it be like this? Am I going to learn how to fake my way through grief when it rears its ugly head?"

Just in time, Genevieve arrived, opened my door, and guided me into her car. I told her, "Geny, I can't shake the sadness! it has taken over my entire body and my mind." We sat in silence for a few moments, then she drove us toward the beach, and we walked through the sands of La Jolla Shores. Within moments of strolling alongside the ocean, I could speak again.

As the months back at work rolled along, I couldn't talk about Emilio while trying to get through my workday. I took on a stoic personality that reminded me of my mother's behavior when she didn't want to deal with me and my childish "little girl" issues. She would often roll her eyes and give me her cold, dismissive look when I came home from school with complaints about the nun who was mean to me or the boy who made fun of my short pixie haircut.

Stoicism is a school of philosophy from ancient Greece and Rome in the early third century BC. It is a philosophy of life that maximizes positive emotions, reduces negative emotions, and helps individuals hone their character virtues. Although this is all very noble, the problem for someone like my mother and myself is that we find ourselves washing over the fact that we are living in severe pain and vulnerability in our attempt at self-preservation. Rather than venting our anger, we pent up our emotions which can be bad for our mental health. The apple doesn't fall far from the tree.

Publicly, I found myself living in an aura of self-control and fortitude, but privately I developed an intense desire never to want the freshness of the pain to deaden. My grief became very personal, very quickly. The pain felt like a bond with Emilio. I didn't feel connected to him if I couldn't feel pain. I couldn't feel alive if I wasn't connected to Emilio. I was appalled that I only felt alive while quietly grieving Emilio, alone. What was I feeling when I was in a conversation with a friend, or when I was presenting a new product to one of my customers? Nothing, absolutely nothing. I was merely trying to get through my day so I could return home and crawl into my bed with my pillow and blankets wrapped around my entire body.

For the first two years, I caught myself sweeping my eyes over a crowd of children. I was still looking for him. At different times in my day, I could not accept his complete and definitive absence.

I dreaded being introduced to anyone new in my life. The thought that someone would ask me if I had children was unbearable. I didn't want to say yes, fearing they would start asking me questions about my child. When someone did ask me this question, I sometimes said "no." This answer came to me out of sheer desperation to escape rather than collapse.

Although I read many books on grief and attended my share of support groups, I navigated my way through my grief journey with the help of my grieving husband—my love, my soulmate, my rock. We patiently accepted that our healing techniques were different from one another.

My way was to seek out grief workshops and mom support groups. Richard wanted to be quiet and introspective. I wanted comfort from others who knew exactly how I felt. Richard assured me that if his methods didn't work and he found himself depressed, he would seek therapy. Spending time with Sierra became Richard's therapy session. He set up a studio in our garage and started making children's furniture. He named his business "Little Wings." He and Sierra would get outdoors for numerous walks each day between creating his pieces. He found his solace with her and his return to nature.

One evening when I returned home from work, Richard shared a story with me. He told me that he and Sierra were walking up the hillside of our neighborhood park, Presidio, a park that had always been a sacred place for us to take walks with Emilio and Sierra.

Richard said, "Out of the blue, Sierra took off up the hill running toward something. I called for her to come back, but she kept on running. Suddenly, she stopped and just stood silently still. Finally catching up to her, I saw her staring at a little boy. He was probably about four or five years old. He had a mop of blond hair and was shouting out for his dad to wait for him. Diane, I was so sad. Sierra thought that he was Emilio. She was running to catch up with him. She turned her body around, and with her head hanging low, she began to wander down the hill, back to me. Watching her was heartbreaking."

After Emilio died, Richard knew that he couldn't go back to working retail in the frame shop, a place where he had worked for the past fifteen years. One morning he said, "I can't talk about it over and over again each day to customers. The pain is much too deep. I know that I can make some income through my furniture sales." I knew that my salary would keep us secure and that his own "Little Wings" business would take off in time. "We will be okay," I assured him. We had no idea then that we would eventually find our way into the world of nonprofit work, enabling Richard to make a solid, gratifying career change.

Returning to work eventually became a welcomed distraction for me. My "workaholic" tendencies helped me cope with my sadness and got me through the day. My job gave me life purpose during my insecure and low self-esteem years. Now, it simply filled up the space every time the pain of grief knocked me off my feet.

Our constant return to nature helped get the two of us through our sorrow. We took long walks on the beach every weekend, hiked the trails at Torrey Pines in La Jolla, and spent most evenings watching the sunset with Sierra by our side. We tried hard to stay in a few moments of peace, but these moments were temporary. Sometimes an entire tranquil experience would change, the moment we switched on the radio station and a song that reminded us of Emilio would play, or when we were on a walk and a five-year-old child would be riding his skateboard straight toward us. Sometimes these experiences would affect both of us simultaneously, and together we tried to catch our breath and lift ourselves out of the abyss we had crawled into. In these moments, rising to stand became an impossible feat.

One chilly fall Sunday morning, Richard and I were sitting on the front porch sipping coffee and catching up on newspaper articles. A young boy, about seven years old, rode by on his skateboard. "Hi, Mr. and Mrs. Nares," he said.

"Remember me. I'm Noah, Emilio's friend from preschool!"

We muttered a quick hello, buried our heads, and hoped that he would move quickly along. With a twinkle in his eye, he smiled and waved goodbye. In an instant, I returned to that unbearable feeling of pain, a pain deep within my heart, and my throat. It suddenly hurt to breathe.

Simply sitting on the patio, enjoying my coffee, distracted by an article in the Style Section of the *New York Times*. There it was, the duality of grief.

There are many moments of unexpectant grief that I remember. Several years after Emilio's death, I witnessed joyful maternal love at two different family gatherings. Although both experiences were beautiful observations of paternal love, the painful aftereffects were excruciating.

Our family had gathered for Thanksgiving Day at John and Nancy Jo's house. I was standing in the kitchen with Nancy Jo and her teenage son, Matthew. The two of them were preparing several of the courses for our Thanksgiving meal. As they gently moved within and around one another, I felt like my heart was breaking all over again. As I watched this beautiful moment unfold, my eyes filled with tears, and the familiar burn I had become accustomed to knowing intimately, would not go away. I remember quietly leaving the kitchen, discreetly choking on my tears. Feeling sorry for myself, I said to Richard, "Nancy Jo and John are so blessed to have these beautiful children. I wish I could just have one of them."

It was a beautiful October afternoon in La Jolla. Richard and I stood off to the side of the ballroom as my brother Michael and his lovely daughter Gia danced together on her wedding day. I was joyous observing my brother's love for his precious little girl. He was so proud of her, as we all were. Within moments, Gia's husband Will joined his mom Gina on the dance floor. They moved so beautifully together; it was clear that they had been dancing with one another Will's entire life.

That damn, unwanted grief showed up once again and sucked all of the air out of the room. Richard gently put his arm around me. He knew that I was suffering. We both realized we were witnessing one of the most captivating moments of a mother and son's life together, a son's wedding day. As tears started streaming down my face, I found myself eager to run and hide before anyone could see me in this state of grief.

We made a mad dash toward the patio door, and out into the garden, where only a few young people were hanging out with champagne and cigarettes. Richard led me to a picnic table to sit and rest. Several moments later I could breathe once again.

Chapter 25
Active Healing

October 2001

One year after Emilio's death, it was a warm October morning, and I was swimming laps at the nearby public pool. My favorite part of my swim was when I was at least 20 minutes into my routine. That's when I entered the zone where I could feel the comfort of slumber just a few breaths away. Thank goodness that I never fell asleep when this happened, but I became so calm that it was almost as if I was smiling my way through a peaceful version of sleep.

I was still having difficulty sleeping at night. I often awoke with nightmares. Most of the time, they were dreams about Emilio standing inches away from me, and every time I reached out to catch him, he would drift away. I kept losing him, and then suddenly, I would wake up and mournfully remember that he really was gone. But when I swam, he was always by my side. When I finished my 50-minute swim, my memories became joyful ones. I was happy because I felt the two of us had shared an uninterrupted peaceful dream.

We first introduced Emilio to swimming when he was two years old. He struggled with fear of the water and would not let go of us. It would take him until he was five years old to show an interest in the sport. We provided him with several swimming lessons by the time he turned four years old.

One day, just after his fifth birthday, Emilio walked to the pool's side and shouted to me, "Hey, Mom, watch!" In an instant, he performed a cannonball dive into the pool. He came up for air and then headed out with a pretty decent freestyle stroke for a five-year-old. He proceeded to swim to the other side of the pool. He exclaimed in a loud, bold voice, "I told you, Mom, that I would swim when I was ready!"

I had witnessed his confidence many times in his short, sweet life. His little face was filled with pride when he accomplished a goal that he had set.

One year after Emilio's death, I arranged to take a series of lessons with a well-respected San Diego swim coach, Deena Schmidt. Deena was a 1972 Olympic Gold Medalist and the Women's Team coach at San Diego State University, my alma mater.

I knew how to swim, but I strongly desired to improve my strokes and breathing. I always had to stop after swimming just one length of the pool. While on a spin bike at the gym, I would watch the Master Swimmers at 7:00 a.m. and marvel at the beauty of their strokes, the ease at which they glided across the pool and back, doing flip turns at each end of the pool.

"I want to do that!" I announced it to Richard one morning.

Deena told me, "One day, you will find yourself not stopping when you reach the end of one lap, then again, and again, you will just keep on going because you have trained yourself to do so."

She was right. One day I just kept on swimming, back and forth, back and forth. When I was in the pool, I felt better than usual. The water became a powerful healing tool. Another day I felt as if Emilio was gliding along on my back. I could feel his breath as he whispered in my ear, "Mommy, you can do this. You will find peace in the water."

I eventually set a goal to swim for one mile three days a week. By the time I reached my goal, I had "out of body" exhilarating experiences while I swam. After the first three-quarters of a mile, I felt like I was sleeping. As dangerous as this sounds, the truth is I always found the end of the pool lane safely to do my turn-around, but the sleeping part was felt while I was in the process of swimming. My mind was awake, but my body was so relaxed that I never realized how much effort it took to continually get from one end of the pool to the other for one hour. It was sheer pleasure, and I often realized I was smiling as I swam across the pool. Every week I yearned to get in the pool.

I read a quote from Diana Nyad after her first attempt to swim from Cuba to Florida. In a 2011 interview with *The New York Times*, she said, "Swimming is the ultimate form of sensory deprivation. You are left alone with your thoughts in a much more severe way, and for many, the only way to find the solitary self, and the internal retreat, is to swim many laps."

She was right. In the pool, no one could bother me. No one could talk to me. Swimming was like being in church or sitting in my therapist's chair. One day, I found myself smiling as I glided along. I was learning how to feel safe and peaceful again. Swimming, for me, became my ultimate form of meditation.

The pool wasn't the only place where I felt Emilio's presence. I soon discovered that Richard had his own miracle stories to share with me.

One morning, which happened to be Good Friday, Richard and Sierra were playing in the alley. He heard my voice calling out to him, "Richard! Richard!" I was in meetings in Los Angeles that morning. Richard swore I was right there in the alley calling out for him numerous times!

One afternoon, two years after Emilio's passing, I was napping on the couch. Like a whisper from eternity, I woke up to his voice saying, "Mommy, mommy, the message is clear: Love is eternal. Know that I am always with you." As his face began to fade away, I soon felt his soft, warm hand gently touch my face, and then, in an instant, he was gone.

Several months after that experience, Emilio appeared to me again in a dream. This time he said, "Mommy, you are changing in ways you have yet to see. You will heal, Mommy. Watch closely. My spirit surrounds you at every turn."

Divine messages started me on the road to healing. Clarity was manifesting in me as I began to understand that it is in the **remembering** and the **knowing** that I will see my son again.

Richard and I began to find ourselves sometimes smiling instead of crying as we watched the sun setting over the ocean. Hundreds of vivid, impactful memories came rolling back into our minds, some of whom we embraced and others we ran away from. We began to move the needle just a bit on the frequency level of when we were suffering versus when we felt joy.

But even so, the duality of grief was always present. I had the choice to release it or bury it. Most often, I chose to bury it to get through my day. It was easier to do than to crawl back into bed and scream into my pillow. But sometimes, I ran straight into it, circling around the matador like a bull in the ring. Like the bull, grief would triumph over my diminished body and blood until, one day, I got back up and knocked that damn emotion right out of my brain. I knew it was time to at least give it my best punch as I tried desperately to get my life back into some kind of decent order.

Chapter 26
Kitchen Table Conversations

One day, returning home from work, Richard and I started the first of what was to become many "Kitchen Table Conversations."

We asked one another, "What do we do now?" We both knew that now we wanted to become strong again. We knew that now the work really begins. The work of recovery—even in the darkest hours, we knew it would still be there.

We loved being parents and felt empty without a child to love. Parenthood has been our role for five years. Our home was hollow, apart from our love for one another and our devoted dog, Sierra. We asked one another, "Who are we now? A seat remained empty at the table. A seat we needed to fill soon, or so I thought."

I was pretty sure I was ready to explore adoption options, but Richard was not at all sure. He had known the greatest love of all, his love of Emilio. He did not think he could love like this again. The thought of something terrible happening to another child of ours was unbearable for him.

"You don't have to do this right now, Mrs. Nares."

I heard those words while on the phone with San Diego adoption attorney Carol Dalton. Carol was very compassionate as she listened to my story. It was an early November morning, two years after Emilio died.

For me, my interest in adoption was very different from Richard's feelings. I could not imagine not being a mother again. I thought that adoption would be the next chapter for us. I believed I was ready to jump into the system. How could I have known how it would feel to hear the words she spoke. Carol said, "Mrs. Nares, please know that you will need to prepare yourself for possible disappointment. Birth mothers change their minds all the time."

She continued, "The child that you fall in love with can be taken away at any time. The newborn you have prepared for might never join your family at all."

I gasped for air at the thought of being faced with this heartbreaking possibility. Carol listened to me sob for several moments, then told me that we could pick up the conversation any time in the future. I quickly thanked her and rushed out of my office to find Richard in his studio. I frantically said, "You're right. I can't do this. I can't risk the feeling of loss and despair once again." Richard wrapped his arms around me as I continued to cry. He soon said, "Maybe we just aren't ready yet. Let's move slowly. I know that we will find our way."

Our home and garden served as significant sanctuaries. They were the places where we could rest and nurture ourselves emotionally, mentally, and spiritually.

Our house was the only home that Emilio knew. Although it felt as if we had spent the last few years with Emilio on a lifeboat that was being tossed around in a stormy, dark sea, our house anchored the three of us.

Taking a long walk on the beach with Richard became a desire for me most evenings. While gazing endlessly out to sea, I reminded myself that this God-given vast creation was so much bigger than me. As my anger with God began to dissipate, a clearer vision and an answer of sorts started to come into play.

The two of us each had a gnawing desire to move away from our grief by doing something to help other people who were suffering. We desperately needed to sink our teeth into something that could make a difference in the world. With personal time on our hands and no children to care for, we dug deep inside ourselves. We soon became amazed at the essential, meaningful conversations developing between us.

Richard was the first one of us to articulate the plan.

He said, "We know the world of childhood cancer intimately. While many organizations are established to raise money for a cure, we could do something to help parents with the day-to-day needs of their child's cancer journey." I knew he was on to something big. I responded with, "Of course, there are so many needs that a family has to navigate through when they hear those debilitating words 'your child has cancer'."

Stepping back into the world of childhood cancer gave us a sense of duty, an advocate's passion for a cause. As I was healing, I felt a fierce calling to let the world know that children get cancer too. We laid out a plan with an overpowering sense of raising awareness about this horrifying injustice.

The businesswoman within me started coming alive again as Richard and I garnered stories of need from the social workers and nurses who cared for Emilio at San Diego Children's Hospital.

Imagine working your way through hearing the words "your child has cancer." Then imagine the hopelessness that you would feel when your doctor tells you your child will need to come to the clinic or hospital once, sometimes twice a week. Now imagine that you do not have a car.

We recalled the many stories we had heard while in the clinic or hospital with Emilio. We remembered the injustice that we witnessed. One of the families was homeless. They lived on the streets with a child who had leukemia—this story and another one in particular haunted us for years to come. A seventeen-year-old high school boy was mugged at the South Bay San Diego trolley station in the afternoon as he returned home from a day of chemotherapy.

As he lay on the ground, he crunched his knees and threw his arms around his chest. He screamed, "Take my wallet, but don't touch my porta-catheter, I had chemo today, and I need it to help me survive!"

A story like this should not go quietly into oblivion. Something needed to be done, and awareness needed to be raised. What I didn't consider was how it would feel to walk back through that hospital door.

Previous to this newly found advocacy role, two years after Emilio's death, I had been to the hospital only once. I attended a bereavement workshop in the oncology unit four months after his loss. I showed up for the first two sessions, but as I tried to leave my house the third week, I couldn't get out the door. My legs wouldn't move. I crawled onto the couch and lay there paralyzed for the rest of the evening.

I couldn't have imagined then that it would take another year and a half before I could step through the hospital door. Richard had arranged an appointment with Victoria Grigg, the Oncology Social Worker who cared for the three of us. As we drove to the hospital in silence, Richard said in a comforting voice, "We can do this. We can walk through those doors and tell Victoria we are ready to offer our support."

Victoria's compassionate, calm voice always brought me back off the ledge whenever Dr. Sudari delivered terrible news to us. She picked us up off the floor more times than I can remember. I adored her and was very excited to tell her about our plans to help the families she cared for daily.

By offering service to others, we eventually healed the constant sadness that lived within us. Here, we found our way to honor Emilio.

Chapter 27
How It All Began

One morning while I was getting ready for work, a call came from a local TV station, Channel 10. A reporter told me that he read an article in the *San Diego Union-Tribune* about Richard driving a local four-year-old boy, Ramon Gonzalez, and his mother to and from Rady Children's Hospital for his chemotherapy treatments.

The reporter also told me that the article referred to Emilio's story and that, together with the San Diego Blood Bank, we had organized the largest bone marrow drive in San Diego's history. This drive was established and sponsored by the San Diego Chargers Football Team as we searched for a donor for Emilio. Over the course of a weekend, thousands of people came out to be tested.

We chatted for a few minutes about how shocked the reporter had been when he read Richard's words that cited how many parents did not have a car and transported their children by public transportation.

The reporter was interested in interviewing Richard within the next two hours. They were to meet at the front door of the hospital. Richard wasn't thrilled about doing the interview. He was a bit of an introvert, or better said, he was a private person, certainly more so than I was.

Richard surprised me with his calm and confident interview. A variety of phone calls quickly followed. Community leaders wanted to know more about the soft-spoken, kind man who wanted to help children in need. He started getting invitations to speak, as well.

I had three years of Toastmasters under my belt, and I loved public speaking, but with my busy job, I knew that my time as a childhood cancer advocate would come eventually. For now, in the early days of the Emilio Nares Foundation (ENF), I was thrilled that Richard could get our work off the ground.

When I wasn't working, I spent time communicating with the staff and adding my input to the development of ENF programs. On the weekends, I volunteered with the families and their children.

During this time, I came across a quote from award-winning journalist and news anchor Diane Sawyer that really inspired me. In an interview, she said, "In the broken places, the light can still shine through. Hope and possibility, the cure in overcoming sadness, is in caring about other people."

She hit it right on the nose.

It was clear that my cure for sadness would come as I cared for other moms and dads. Richard and I had landed right where we were supposed to be.

Yes, my heart ached every time I saw a child with an IV pole attached to their shirt, but I calmed myself by thinking of Emilio. If he could face so much adversity, I could rise above my discomfort and help heal another parent's heart.

I have always been conscious that there would be moms and dads who did not want to talk to me. My child died.

Like myself, they wanted to speak with someone whose child survived this dreadful diagnosis. They wanted hope, not uncertainty. During Emilio's three years with cancer, I only wanted to talk with Claudia, or Susan, the parent liaisons whose children survived. The oncology parent liaison team included two parents whose children had not survived.

I was the soldier on the battlefield who wanted to know that we would absolutely get to the other side of this nightmare with our son. We knew we would wake up one morning and find Emilio's cancer gone for good. I wanted to speak to a parent whose story resulted in a way just like my story would end; my son would be healed.

Surprisingly, my calls were always returned. There were moms who wanted to talk to me. Moms often told me they were comforted by me because they knew that I had so much to teach them about the day-in, day-out conflicts they were facing.

I still wore my heart on my sleeve, as I had done most of my life, but now I was empathetic in a way I had never known. Although I could feel their pain, I wasn't taking it home with me.

The suffering that comes from losing one's child is brutally extreme. It appeared that now, my child was making sure I had a pass—a "hall pass" of sorts, an excuse or a reason to be protected, perhaps so my heart could heal. I was beginning to live without being in a constant state of desperation.

Business and community leaders started inviting Richard to speak. At one of the local non-profit luncheons, we met Mr. Michael Aragon, whose organization provided grants to grassroots or emerging organizations that serve low-income Latino communities. Mr. Aragon had spent his career in healthcare and started his foundation so that he could assist other like-minded non-profits. After hearing Richard speak, Mr. Aragon came over to our table to introduce himself.

The conversation that followed prompted us to realize that we needed to become a non-profit organization so that we could raise funds. Mr. Aragon's guidance and experience gave us a clear picture of what we needed to do. He paid our attorney fees so that we could receive our non-profit 501(c)(3) status.

With this status in place, he gave us our first grant. Now, we could officially begin helping families.

Our mission statement began and continues to this day: "The Emilio Nares Foundation helps families navigate through their child's journey with cancer and ensures that no child misses a cancer treatment due to lack of transportation." One of the original board members was Dr. Luz Quiroga. The Quiroga's were the first family whom Richard and I counseled when we returned to the hospital in our new role as "Childhood Cancer Advocates."

Luz, her husband Jorge, their oldest son Nicolas, and their four-year-old son Martin came into our lives one year after Emilio's passing. Martin had just relapsed from ALL leukemia. Luz was looking for someone to talk to about the bone marrow transplant journey as an option for Martin. Unfortunately, Nicolas was not a match for Martin.

When Luz tells the story of how we met one another, she leads in with the words of social worker Victoria Grigg: "You need to talk to Diane Nares."

"That's what I heard after my son Martin was diagnosed with cancer," said Dr. Quiroga (Luz). "Victoria continued to tell me that Richard and Diane Nares created the largest bone marrow drive in San Diego. It was a way for Diane to channel her grief because it had been almost a year since Emilio passed away."

For the first time, I told our story publicly at Luz's church, St. Pius X, in Chula Vista.

Immediately after Nicolas' results showed that he was not a match for Martin, the Bone Marrow Registry search began. Gratefully, after a few short months, the Quiroga's found a match on the registry for Martin. Luz's question for us was, "What U.S. hospital is the best place for us to take Martin for his transplant?"

Richard and I believed strongly that finding a children's hospital that had done the most pediatric bone marrow transplants was essential. We wanted to go where the specialists had seen everything that could happen to a child during a transplant. San Diego Children's Hospital provided us with impeccable, exceptional care during Emilio's cancer treatments, but their bone marrow transplant unit was just beginning at that time.

The Quiroga's chose Seattle Children's Hospital, one of the hospitals we visited with Emilio. It was closer to home than Boston, where we had traveled for Emilio's transplant.

Martin underwent a successful transplant in 2002. He has had his share of complications and specific side effects that will always be concerning for Luz and Jorge but miraculously, Martin is cancer-free!

Richard and I flew to Seattle to spend a few days with the Quiroga family. Martin was halfway through his posttransplant timeframe and the entire family welcomed us into their world. One afternoon, I accompanied Luz to the local Walmart to purchase t-shirts for Martin.

Luz and I were gradually becoming trusted friends. We were two moms who shared a common life of devotion to our little boys. As we were riding up the hospital elevator to return to Martin's room, Luz told me that she would be very happy to carry a baby for Richard and me if having a baby is something we would like to do.

Upon hearing her generous words, my legs soon crumbled beneath me. It was an all too familiar feeling, reminiscent of two other times when my legs could no longer hold me in place. I knew it was a matter of my body moving into a place of unbelievable shock. This happened the first time I heard, "Emilio has leukemia." The second time, we were standing in line at the Starbucks in Boston Logan Airport, soon to board our flight back to San Diego. Emilio's tiny casket was boarding a different plane than ours. My body could not sustain my grief. As I collapsed to the ground, I soon felt the gentle arms of Nancy Jo lifting me up and guiding me into the nearest seat in the waiting area. And now, here I was, in the elevator at Seattle Children's Hospital, trying to get back to Martin's bone marrow transplant unit.

As Luz swooped me up, all the despair of the past four years embraced my entire body, mind, and heart. Luz and I grabbed a couple of chairs in a waiting area and began to talk. "Luz," I gently said. "Perhaps you don't know that I am already 48. Your offer to carry our baby is incredibly beautiful and an act of extraordinary generosity. I do not think that raising another child is what God and Emilio have planned for me. I do know that my higher purpose is to serve other children and their families through this horrifying journey of childhood cancer. That is what we will do with our lives. Thank you, Luz and Martin, for allowing us to be a part of your family as you continue on this transformative journey."

Luz bowed her head to hide her tears, and the two of us hugged one other tightly. We were officially bonded for life, the two of us. Luz joined us in the mission of ENF and has made it her life work. She is truly and genuinely the heart and soul of the organization.

When Martin was thirteen-years-old, he was interviewed by my friend Elizabeth Ireland. At that time, Liz's career background was in TV journalism and communications, most prominently in PR management. She was the first professional to assist me in the very early stages of writing my book about Emilio's life in 2012. In an interview, Martin told Liz:

"Having cancer so young, I don't remember most of it. I was just a kid. I only remember the good things, like when Mr. Richard and Ms. Diane visited me during my transplant. I remember the wonderful nurses always smiling and my parents and brother always there for me. It's human nature to only remember the good things. My mom raised me without any restrictions or handicaps. The doctors told her, 'You don't want to raise a child that everyone would feel sorry for.'

I am really thankful for that. It's safe to say kids who go through this become more mature. My brother tells me that I speak like an old man! It lends to a different understanding of the world.

I have lost some friends in the past, and that's never a fun thing. My friend David and I went to SAT prep class the entire summer, so I saw him every day. Then I found out through a Facebook message that he had passed away. I hung out with him a lot. The fact that I never received word from a human being and heard from a third-party source like Facebook was crushing. I just lost it. Of course, it wasn't the first time, but it's always hard.

There is a burden with being a cancer survivor. Countless times you will ask yourself, 'Why am I here and other people aren't?' Even though you have the same disease or maybe something worse than somebody else.

I cope with that by seeing the smiles on other people's faces. A friend in ceramics class asked me, 'Why do you stay so positive?' I told her I don't do it for myself; I do it for others. Your positivity could be enough to brighten somebody's day or inspire them to achieve something great. I know what's happened. I see what other people go through. To always stay positive is something I strive to do. There is always something to be happy about. That's been my driving force ever since I had cancer."

On April 29, 2020, Martin graduated from college. He is an exceptional young man who will go out into the world doing good work, just like his mom, dad, and brother.

Luz has shown her appreciation for the two of us numerous times in our lives. Even though I didn't get to work within ENF every day with the rest of the staff, Luz introduced me to everyone. She would say, "This is Diane Nares, co-founder of the Emilio Nares Foundation and, most importantly, Emilio's mom."

Chapter 28
Richard's Epic Runs

Since 2011 Richard has gone on to run multiple marathons every year since his first Boston Marathon, which honored Emilio's life. He raised funds and awareness for the programs of ENF with his first two Epic Runs. In the summer of 2011, Richard ran from Los Angeles to San Diego. Then in 2013, he ran from San Francisco to San Diego.

Later that year, Richard was chosen to be a CNN Hero. He made it to the Top 100 Global Heroes, then into the Top 10. President Obama selected the Emilio Nares Foundation video to be featured on CNN that year.

In 2018 Richard ran from Seattle, Washington, to San Diego. He ran 15 miles every morning and 15 miles every afternoon. The trip took him two-and-a-half months that summer.

Richard and his 2018 run consisted of a team of dedicated runners and volunteers cared for by the irreplaceable Lynn Ellenberg. With the help of her husband, Sholom Ellenberg, Lynn, my niece, and Goddaughter, handled every detail while on the road. Lynn was so thorough that all Richard had to do was run! Just like Forrest

Gump, Richard kept on running every day. Because of Lynn, he didn't have to worry about anything else.

The passionate team of 2018 stopped to visit nine children's hospitals along the way. They delivered ENF's unique Loving Tabs Shirts to children in treatment. These shirts were designed and crafted by Luz and her cousin to facilitate access to medical devices without requiring a scared child to remove their garment. The shirts make pediatric treatment a little bit easier by providing comfort and dignity for the children.

I never thought I would want to run a half marathon, but on November 8, 2015, that is exactly what I did.

Taking up running had nothing to do with proving something to myself or losing my son Emilio. Running was just an opportunity to return to a form of exercise I practiced many years ago. However, five miles were the most miles I had ever run back then. A half marathon is 13.2 miles, and it was daunting to me. I took on the challenge but couldn't have predicted that I would learn much about grief while running.

A San Diego running group chose the Emilio Nares Foundation as their charity to support. They named themselves Cheetah Charity Runners. Today, they are called the Cheetah Charity Running Group. The team of 50 runners, all local professionals in various careers, became an instant family to Richard, myself, and ENF. Also on my team were three special women in my life, Elizabeth Ireland, Dominique Coulon, and our ENF Development Director, Heidi Cramer. These three lovely women were the best of friends, and I felt honored to train with them for my first half marathon. We ran together with the other inspirational women and men of CCR, but our training took place only three days a week, because our jobs left us little time for further discipline. However, we had five months before the Big Sur Half Marathon in Monterey, California. The Monterey Half Marathon was the perfect choice because it was between Big Sur and Carmel, two of my favorite places.

I was diligent in my training, never missing one practice run with the team. Our training consisted of pre-sessions on nutrition, stretching, healing tools for soreness, and the power of mental fitness. I managed to get myself from running one mile to an eventual 11.5-mile training run twice in my training schedule. Our dear friend, Dr. Chad Wells, Sports Medicine Specialist and owner of The League Sports Rehab, came out to do some healing work on us whenever the need arose, which was often in those six months of training.

Becoming a runner allowed me to share my training runs with my sister Teresa who started running years before me and impressively ran a half marathon annually. Teresa and her husband, Dave Kaupke, were members of the San Diego Track Club, as was Richard. Not only did they spend Saturday early mornings together training, but Richard became Teresa's coach as she aspired to run a faster pace. She was a beautiful runner and inspired me tremendously. From her, I learned determination, grit, and grace could all be experienced through running.

This physical challenge that loomed in front of me occurred 15 years after Emilio's passing. By the first day of November, I felt like I blinked, and it was race day.

Throughout the first nine miles, I felt energized and joyful. The sun was shining, and I was having a fantastic time! The half-marathon route was absolutely breathtaking. We passed live music at nearly every mile marker along a rolling course that hugged the ocean. We saw otters floating on their backs, cracking open oysters and the seals swimming parallel to the road acted as our natural pacers. Wow, my first race! What a rush! It seemed like the entire Monterey Bay community lined the streets to cheer us on. Their energy inspired me, and their signs made me laugh.

I stayed slow and steady as Richard taught me to do. My ultra-marathon running husband surprised me by announcing he'd be running with me the morning of the race. I didn't think he'd have the patience to go that slow because his walk was certainly faster than my jog, but he stayed by my side the entire time. I had no way of knowing how important that would be.

As I approached mile 10, my legs stopped moving. They felt like concrete blocks. Everything slowed down and seemed to move at a glacial pace. I remember saying to myself repeatedly, "Oh my god. I cannot go on. My body cannot do this. I do not have the strength or conditioning to go forward. I was foolish to think I could run a half marathon, 13.2 miles!"

I now know why Richard didn't tell me that most runners "hit the wall" at some point. I would have become anxious, scared, and worried, so he kept that imminent reality to himself. It wasn't as if I stopped, I was still moving my feet, but they felt like two tiny blocks trying to push a colossal truck uphill. Eventually, I was grounded in place, unable to move. This run was becoming more than tough: I started gasping for air—this was beyond the bounds of "hitting a wall."

I immediately recognized that grief again took control of my mind and body. I did not have a mantra planned for this long run, but a phrase developed in my broken mind, and within a moment, I was repeating to myself, "If I can endure the loss of my only child, then I can do THIS."

Over and over again, these words propelled me into survival mode: "If I can endure the loss of my only child, then I can do THIS."

Soon after, I could not stop sobbing. Grief was stuck in my throat, and I could no longer breathe. As I began to hyperventilate, I strained to get the words out. "It's grief, I know it's grief, I know this feeling so well," I told Richard.

I desperately tried to find air. Richard encouraged me to walk slowly and take deep breaths. He put his warm arm around my shoulders and gently repeated the words, "Walk slowly and breathe deeply. You will catch your breath again. Just keep on breathing."

In what felt like an eternity, but in reality, was probably about 60 seconds, I did start to breathe again in a normal rhythm. I regained strength in my legs and started to pick up my pace. I thought about how suffering through this race is nothing compared to what Emilio endured. My son's combination of chemotherapy and a bone marrow transplant is like running a full marathon and then getting in the ring with Mike Tyson for a knockout punch.

I finally got my groove back at some point during mile 11. I knew I was back in a safe place with the capacity to conquer this beast. I ran my heart out the last two miles. I pushed against the human and natural feeling of despair and wanting to give up, just as I had after Emilio left this earth.

Richard and I shared an emotional goodbye as he gave me away to the finish line. As he started to step back toward the crowd, I remember shouting, "No, don't go. Please help me cross!" I then heard his words, "You don't need me, Diane. You've got this. You trained for it, you can overcome any obstacle in your life, and you've conquered the most important one already, your son's passing. This finish line is right in front of you. Go get it!"

He blew a kiss as I crossed over. And there he was.

I ended strong but learned a weighty lesson from my half marathon. I stood there shell-shocked, a medal around my neck.

"Grief" was then and continues today to be a big part of my identity. It isn't something that disappears in time. Grief remains with us as we sort through the various events of our lives. For me, it lays quietly dormant until the next devastating life challenge smashes right into me.

My equilibrium is most often rocked when someone I love becomes very sick. Then, I get the reminder we cannot control so many pieces of our life experiences. Reliving the feelings of loss and pain is the chance we take when we decide to embrace our lives, love others fully, and face our fears.

Some semblance of grief is buried deep within me nearly two decades later. I have discovered from my sports of choice; running and swimming release the pain and the memories that I have pushed down so far within me to survive the day.

Running and swimming became the solo acts that left me alone with my thoughts to bring about my memories of Emilio. While amid both activities, I could flush out the grief and feel my loss on a deeper level. Richard talks about how "one's mind has time" when running. It's easy to push grief down during your day-to-day life moments, but running moves it forward.

That day of my half marathon, I didn't realize I'd be running right into my grief. Grief, that monster, that intruder, reminded me once again that I will never *not* grieve the death of my son. There will never not be a finish line to cross. I will always return to the inferno of his physical loss from my life. As long as I am living, I will know the depths of my loss because my sadness equals my love for him. A mother's love for her child is immense and overwhelmingly powerful. My loss of Emilio is a vast indescribable hole, as if part of my heart is left empty.

Grief never goes away. It lingers there, somewhere within each of us, until a moment such as my half-marathon occurs. A memory pops into our minds. We hear a particular song on the radio, a movie flashes across the TV screen, and we scramble to turn the channel before facing the pain of how that feels to see something so hauntingly familiar.

I remind myself that although it didn't start out that way, completing this half marathon was necessary to help me continue my lifelong road to recovery. Intense exercise can either take us to a place of remembering our loss with sadness or it can inspire us to wrap our arms around our grief and teach ourselves how to live within it.

Chapter 29
Those Who Do the Healing

When any family faces a cancer diagnosis, the relationship they build with their oncologist should be mutual respect, trust, and love. We had that every step of the way. It began with the skilled and compassionate pediatric hematology/oncology team at Rady Children's Hospital, San Diego. Our final relationship was with Dr. Eva Guinan. Although her Phase 2 Study did not keep Emilio alive, there was never a moment of doubt about taking Emilio to Boston Children's Hospital. There was a 50/50 chance that the Haplo-Identical Transplant with Richard as a donor would work.

Eva and her team did everything they could for Emilio. We would have traveled anywhere in the world to save his life. Yes, it was high-risk, but accepting that Emilio was going to die was never an option for us when there was an opportunity available in Boston.

We have the deepest respect for Dr. Guinan and her team, and we will always be grateful to them for how they treated our son. Several months after Emilio died, I received a letter from this compassionate doctor who cared for my son.

"Dear Diane, in the course of being a doctor, I am sure similarly with any other role, there are people and events that touch you more than others, people you remember differently. When I was a resident and first-year fellow, I took over the care of a little boy who went on to die of myelodysplasia. He was the patient, and they were the family who really allowed me to understand that I had what it took to do this. Every time I tell his story I cry, both because of what happened to him but also because of what he gave to me.

Later in my training, I took care of a wonderful teenage girl with horrible Hodgkin's disease. I had to leave for the weekend (my mother was dying), and the girl was also dying in the hospital. I was completely torn about where to be. Defying all expectations, my patient stayed alive in the hospital all weekend. I arrived there straight from the airport at about 11:30 p.m. and went immediately to her room, asking her parents to leave me with her for a while so I could talk to her. She died fifteen minutes after we spoke. She was also my teacher.

There are more stories but the number who teach the most profound lessons is few. Sometimes it is the patient, sometimes it is the parents. In your case, Emilio was the obvious product of an enormous amount of love, but it was the vision and dedication that you and Richard brought to his care that touched us all so deeply and motivates me so much."

Decades later, I am comforted by Dr. Guinan's words. Do I appreciate her validation? Sure.

Did we make the right choice to go to Boston instead of taking Emilio home to die after his second relapse? Absolutely.

The strength of our marriage showed up as grace within the pain. It still does. Ours is a love story, through and through. The result of this love story was Emilio.

As time moves forward, I find myself on some days wanting to dig back into the pain, if only to remember Emilio's face and never to forget the sound of his laughter.

Emilio was my teacher, and I remember him every day of my life.

With each new day, the sun's vital rays nurture me, and light returns to renew my strength. I hope that others who suffer loss can find some peace in the abundant memories that will resurface throughout the rest of their lives.

In time, living a life of service to others diminished my sadness by taking it down several notches. Caring for others can be a beautiful distraction from our suffering. In challenging moments, we find comfort in looking beyond ourselves.

This book is the story of a very special little boy whose life inspired a movement. Emilio's legacy will live on to ensure that one day all children everywhere have a safe, reliable way to get to and from the hospital where they receive their cancer care.

Although Emilio is no longer physically with me, his spiritual presence continues to influence my actions and enhance my broader thinking. My profound loss of him has led me to understand better something deep within me that would protect me all along.

The life script we're given eventually comes full circle as we grow in time to be the best version of ourselves that we can be. Emilio taught me how to aspire toward this transformation.

A life of reflection is an ongoing process, and nothing about it is easy. But the healing comes from learning that my life purpose was to be Emilio's mother and to share him with the world.

It takes an inexhaustible nature to turn tragedy into positive change.

We accomplish this with the help of many people who, through tireless effort, continue to keep our vision and the mission of ENF at the forefront of each new day. We are grateful to ENF's, Luz Quiroga, the Board of Directors, and the dedicated and compassionate staff who carry on Emilio's legacy.

As we happily transition into our future with other projects that raise awareness and funds for ENF, Richard and I are comforted to know that so many families and children will be cared for throughout Southern California.

The Emilio Nares Foundation is a mission of love and hope.

To learn more, visit the website: www.enfhope.org

Epilogue

September 2, 2022

I am often asked, "What does the title of your book mean?"

The answer to this question is generated from the fact that Emilio left behind a variety of examples of his artistic talents. One of them was his interest in wood making. When Emilio turned four, his birthday wish was to receive the Wood-Carving Tools Pack that he saw one day while browsing through one of Richard's home improvement magazines. The pack included a tool belt which he wore most days during that year. One day when Emilio was two years old, I was polishing our dinner table, just as the early morning light rushed in and pushed itself across the table. In that moment, it allowed me to see more clearly that he had been using his tiny fork to carve little drawings into our Tuscan Farmhouse wood table. This was the table that Richard made shortly after we moved into our first home. Richard's homemade table was placed perfectly between the two arched windows in our 1927 Spanish Bungalow dining room.

Emilio sat at the head of the table, and the two of us sat on opposite sides of him.

It seems impossible to me now that we didn't see these particular artistic creations sooner, but the style of farmhouse furniture that Richard created is referred to as "destressed" which characteristically has a worn, rough look to it. Once we found these special tiny markings, we realized that little by little over time, he had been defining his ownership of the place where he would always sit and have meals with his mom and dad. He didn't have other brothers and sisters whom he could bounce around with, and exchange seats with, like the busy chaos that Richard and I had experienced with our siblings for so many years. For Emilio, it was just him, and this seat was his seat.

For me, it was just Emilio, and he would always have a place at the table.

Twenty-two years after Emilio's death, many things have changed.

Three years ago, I retired from the wine industry after a 30-year career, and Richard stepped back from his 16-year Executive Director's role at the Emilio Nares Foundation.

We both continue to advocate for the organization, and I serve on the event committee for our annual food and wine fundraiser, Harvest for Hope.

In the world of childhood cancer, I still find my most genuine sense of purpose when I am comforting a mom on the cancer journey with her child or speaking with a mom whose child did not survive.

Retirement brought the two of us the gift of time. This was a gift whose power and joy could have never made sense to us until that time came.

I knew that if I could just get him on that plane, Richard would soon understand that the gift of travel, time, and art would transform us both. In the winter of December 2018, we headed to Rome and Paris for Christmas, New Year's Eve, and what would have been Emilio's 23rd birthday, January 6. The trip also served as a 25th wedding anniversary celebration, a celebration which never happened on the proper day of June 19, 2018. On that day, Richard was participating in his "Epic Run" from Seattle to San Diego, and I stayed home, working and taking care of our beautiful rescue dog, Gracey.

This European adventure was the trip of a lifetime. The creative energy that has transpired from the two of us since our vacation transformed our lives.

Richard returned to his true passion for landscape Plein air painting, and I started writing this book, "His Place at the Table." My book wasn't easy to write, and it isn't easy to talk about, but I needed to write it for Emilio, all of those who loved him, and the many children worldwide who suffer from cancer.

I hope that my book will offer some comfort to those who have lost a loved one. I dream that others will be able to tap into moments of respite, despite the permanent ache of their loved one's forever absence. It takes time to grieve and time to heal. When a bereaved person gives themselves permission to take some necessary time for themselves, there will be moments when what seemed impossible will become possible.

As I move into the current state of happiness, I cannot help thinking about the topic of suffering and how it can bind humanity and even be an exquisite vehicle for connection.

I never intend to tell grieving individuals that their sadness will go away. It never goes away. The tragic loss of Emilio from my physical life is still present. My heart continues to ache when I think about all of the missed milestones that we have not and will not ever experience. I will never see my son graduate from high school or college. I will never get the chance to celebrate his business accomplishments, dance with him at his wedding, or hold his baby, my grandchild. There are still moments when I can't even breathe, and all I want to do is get back into bed and hide. However, the ability to get back up and begin moving once again can happen and does happen. In that place of motion, I can breathe again, connect with Emilio, and feel the assurance that many hopeful and joyful moments are within my reach. I willingly begin again to embrace the beauty of living.

Two days after writing this epilogue, President Biden announced that the US/Mexican borders have reopened, as we find ourselves in the middle of the second year of the Covid-19 pandemic.

Yesterday, I received my monthly email from Rosa. Rosa still lives in Tijuana and every month since Emilio died, she came to visit us until the pandemic hit in 2020. She wrote, "Diana, buenos días, finalmente la frontera se ha abierto!" Translated, "The border has reopened!"

We set a date for her to spend time with us. She will come and bring Rosita, who now has two baby boys. We will watch them play in Emilio's backyard playhouse with tears in our eyes. This is the playhouse Emilio helped his daddy build. It still stands strong amongst the flowers and plants of our garden. We will share our stories of what it was like to love Emilio.

Always, Emilio.